1627
Published in the USA 1995 by JG Press
Distributed by World Publications, Inc
Copyright © 1994 by Colour Library Books Ltd, Godalming, Surrey
All rights reserved
No part of this book may be reproduced or transmitted in any
form or by any means, electronic or mechanical, including
photocopying, recording, or by any information storage and
retrieval system, without permission in writing from the Publisher.
Printed and Bound in Singapore
ISBN 1-57215-014-9

The JG Press imprint is a trademark of JG Press, Inc.
455 Somerset Avenue
North Dighton, MA 02764

CHOCOLATE
COOKING

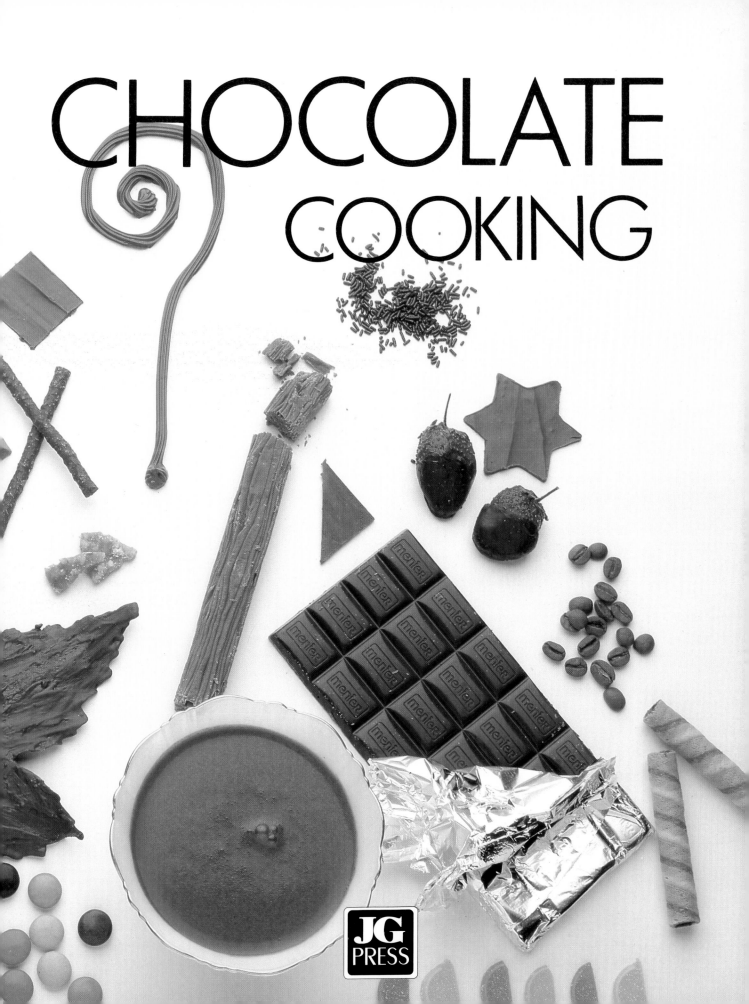

JG
PRESS

Chocolate Roulade (above),
Devil's Food Cake (right) and
Family Chocolate Cake (far
right).

Contents

Introduction

Rich, dark and luxuriously smooth and enticing, chocolate remains one of the most popular ingredients for both everyday and exotic desserts, cakes and confectionery. This section combines a wealth of mouth-watering creations that have been specially selected for their variety as well as their relative ease of preparation: recipes which are bound to delight all those with a passion for chocolate cuisine.

Hints For Cooking With Chocolate
The amount of cocoa butter added to chocolate determines how the chocolate can be used.

Cooking Chocolate
This is not to be confused with cake covering. Cooking chocolate has some cocoa butter replaced with palm kernel oil or coconut oil. Flavorings are used to make the chocolate less expensive and easy to use; it can be used for any chocolate cooking or decoration.

Milk Chocolate
This is rarely used in cooking as it does not give a strong enough flavor, but it can be used for making Easter Eggs and in other recipes that require a delicate flavor.

Couverture
This is a chocolate containing a high proportion of cocoa butter, which gives it a smooth, glossy appearance. Couverture chocolate requires repeated heating and cooling, or tempering; a professional method of working with chocolate.

White Chocolate
This variety has a relatively high sugar content. It is used in some recipes but great care should be taken when using this as it is difficult to melt and has a tendency to go grainy if overheated.

Semi-Sweet Chocolate
This chocolate has a rich, dark flavor and is used in most recipes where chocolate is called for. Semi-sweet eating chocolate can always be used but there are also some varieties available which are specially recommended for cooking.

Bitter Chocolate
This is not easy to buy but it can be made as required. To make plain chocolate bitter add 1 tsp instant coffee powder or granules (or 1 tsp cocoa powder) for every 2oz of chocolate.

Chipped and Grated Chocolate
Chocolate can be chipped and grated either manually or in a food

processor. When grating chocolate, refrigerate for 30 minutes, then hold the chocolate with kitchen paper to prevent it from melting.

Cocoa Powder and Drinking Chocolate
Often used in baking but make sure the lumps are removed. It is best used blended with hot (not boiling) water, so that it forms a smooth paste. Add the paste to the recipe as required.

Melting Chocolate
This should be done carefully as it is particularly important. Break the chocolate into pieces and put in a bowl over a pan of simmering water, or into the top of a double boiler if you have one. When using an electric cooker turn off the heat once the water has boiled. Make sure the bowl fits well into the saucepan so that no steam or water goes into the chocolate. Note: if the chocolate goes solid add a little vegetable oil and beat well.

Microwave Melting
This is a clean and easy way to work with chocolate. Break the chocolate into pieces and put into a suitable bowl. Cover with plastic wrap and melt following the manufacturers instructions. The timing will depend on the quantity of chocolate and the size of the bowl.

Decorating with Chocolate
Chocolate for Dipping
This chocolate has a high proportion of vegetable fat and is less expensive than couverture. Melt the chocolate, which you may find easier to use if you add 1 tblsp of vegetable oil to every 6oz of chocolate.

Chocolate Leaves
These are made by using rose leaves, although any leaves with good strong veins can be used. *Make sure that the leaves you select are not poisonous.* Wash and dry the leaves thoroughly, melt the chocolate and, using a small paintbrush, brush the underside of the leaves with the chocolate. Alternatively you can dip the undersides of the leaves in the chocolate, then place them on non-stick silicone paper or wax paper, chocolate side up. When the chocolate is hard peel off the leaves.

Chocolate Curls
Make sure the chocolate is neither too warm, as it will be too soft to hold a cult, nor too cold, since it will become brittle and may crumble. Using a small knife or even a vegetable peeler make curls by gently shaving the chocolate with the blade.

Craque
To produce these glamorous, long curls, melt the chocolate and spread it with a palette knife onto an ungreased, laminated or marble surface. The chocolate should be ¼ inch thick. Leave it to set, then scrape it up in curls by holding a knife at an angle of 45° and pushing it away from you.

Shapes
To make shapes, melt and pour the chocolate onto an ungreased, laminated or marble surface then, when set, cut into shapes with a sharp knife.

Cakes and Gateaux

Chocolate Fudge Cake

PREPARATION TIME: 15 minutes

COOKING TIME: 45-50 minutes

OVEN TEMPERATURE: 325°F

MAKES: 1 cake, 9 inches in diameter

1¾ cups regular flour
1 tsp bicarbonate of soda
1 tsp baking powder
2½ tblsp cocoa powder
10 tblsp brown sugar
2½ tblsp corn syrup
2 eggs
⅔ cup oil
1¼ cups milk

Chocolate Frosting
6oz semi-sweet chocolate, grated
2½ tblsp light cream

To Decorate
Chocolate shavings

Grease and line a 9 inch cake pan. Sieve the dry ingredients together in a bowl and add the sugar. Make a well in the center and add the syrup, eggs, oil and the milk. Beat them all together until smooth. Pour the cake mixture into the cake pan. Bake in the oven for 45 minutes. When cooked, leave the cake in the pan for a few minutes before turning it out onto a wire rack. To make the frosting: heat the chocolate and cream in a small, heavy saucepan until melted. Cool the mixture slightly and pour over the cake; drag the surface with a fork when it is nearly dry, and decorate with the chocolate shavings.

Chocolate Spice Cake

PREPARATION TIME: 30 minutes

COOKING TIME: 40-50 minutes

OVEN TEMPERATURE: 350°F

MAKES: 1 cake, 8 inches in diameter

5 eggs, separated
¾ cup sugar
3oz semi-sweet chocolate, melted
¾ cup flour
½ tsp ground nutmeg
½ tsp ground cinnamon

½ tsp ground cloves

Cinnamon Topping
Ground cinnamon
Confectioner's sugar

Butter and line a 8 inch spring form cake pan with wax paper (use a pan that has a central funnel). Brush the paper with melted butter and dust with flour. Put the egg yolks and sugar into a mixing bowl and beat them well until the mixture will fall from the whisk in a thick ribbon. Stir in the melted chocolate. Sieve together the flour, nutmeg, cinnamon and cloves, and fold into the cake mixture. Beat the egg whites until stiff but not dry. Gently fold in the beaten egg whites, a little at a time. Pour the mixture into the pan. Bake in a pre-heated oven for 40-50 minutes, or until a skewer inserted into the middle comes out clean. Remove the cake from the oven and let it cool in the pan on a wire rack, for 10 minutes. Turn the cake out to

This page: Chocolate Fudge Cake (top) and Chocolate Almond Cake (bottom).

Facing page: Chocolate Spice Cake (top) and Chocolate Potato Cake (bottom).

Chocolate Roulade (above) and
Chocolate Orange Cake (right).

ool completely. Dust the top of
e cake with a little ground
nnamon and/or confectioner's
ar.

Chocolate Roulade

PREPARATION TIME: 35 minutes
COOKING TIME: 15-20 minutes
OVEN TEMPERATURE: 350°F
MAKES: 1 roulade, 9 inches long

4 tblsp instant coffee
4 tblsp hot water
z semi-sweet chocolate, chopped or
grated
eggs, separated
cup fine sugar

To Decorate
1¼ cups heavy cream
Confectioner's sugar

Grease and line a 13x9 inch jelly
roll pan. Mix the coffee with the
hot water and add the chocolate;
stand in a bowl over a saucepan of
hot water and stir until the
chocolate has melted. Allow the
mixture to cool. Beat together the
egg yolks and sugar until thick,
then fold into the chocolate
mixture. Beat the egg whites until
stiff but not dry, and fold lightly
into the mixture. Pour the mixture
into the prepared pan. Bake in the
oven for 15-20 minutes.
Immediately after taking the cake
out of the oven, cover the cake in
its pan with a damp tea towel, and
leave it to stand overnight. To

decorate: carefully turn the cake
out onto a sheet of wax paper
which has been sprinkled with
confectioner's sugar; remove the
lining paper. Whip the cream until
it holds its shape and spread over
the cake (reserve a little for
decorating). Roll up the cake like a
jelly roll, and dust it with icing
sugar. Decorate the remaining
cream down the center or around
the roulade.

Chocolate Orange Cake

PREPARATION TIME: 30 minutes
COOKING TIME: 40 minutes
OVEN TEMPERATURE: 350°F
MAKES: 1 cake, 8 inches in
diameter

2 cups regular flour
9 tblsp cocoa powder
1 cup butter
1¼ cups fine sugar
2 eggs, beaten
1 cup buttermilk

Frosting
1 cup butter
Grated rind of 1 orange
½ cups confectioner's sugar, sieved
Juice of ½ an orange

To Decorate
Fresh orange segments or slices

Grease and line two 8 inch cake
pans. Sieve together the cocoa and
the flour. Cream the butter and
sugar together until light and fluffy;
gradually add the beaten eggs. Stir
the buttermilk into the mixture,
and then fold in the cocoa and
flour. Turn the mixture into the
prepared pans. Bake for 40
minutes. Remove the cakes from
the oven; turn out of the pans and
allow to cool on a wire rack. When
the cakes are cold, split each cake
into two layers. To make the
frosting: cream the butter with the
orange rind until soft; beat in the
confectioner's sugar, alternately
with the orange juice. Sandwich
the cakes together with some of
the butter frosting and spread the
remaining frosting on the top and
the sides of the cake. "Rough" with
a fork and decorate with the
orange slices or segments.

Austrian Sachertorte

PREPARATION TIME: 40 minutes
plus cooling time

COOKING TIME: 1 hour
15 minutes

OVEN TEMPERATURE: 350°F

MAKES: 1 cake, 8 inches in
diameter

Torte

5oz dark semi-sweet chocolate, grated
1 tblsp warm water
10 tblsp butter
10 tblsp confectioner's sugar
5 eggs, separated
1¼ cups regular flour
1½ tsp baking powder
1oz cornstarch
1 tblsp rum, or strong black coffee
5 tblsp sieved apricot jam

Frosting

½ cup heavy cream
2 tsp brandy
4oz dark semi-sweet chocolate, grated
2oz sweet chocolate, grated
Confectioner's sugar to dust

Grease and flour an 8 inch round cake pan. Melt the chocolate in a basin with the warm water. Cream the butter and confectioner's sugar together until light and fluffy. Beat in the chocolate gradually. Beat in the egg yolks one at a time. Sieve together the flour and the cornstarch and fold it into the chocolate mixture. Beat the egg whites until stiff but not dry. Beat third of the egg whites into the mixture then fold in the remainder Spoon the mixture into the prepared cake pan. Bake for 50 minutes to 1 hour, until firm to the touch. Turn out and cool on a wire rack. Split the cake in half horizontally, sprinkle with rum or coffee, and sandwich together with 2 tblsp apricot jam. Place the cake on a wire rack. Brush all over with the remaining jam. To make the frosting: place the cream in a

Chocolate and Almond Cake

PREPARATION TIME: 45 minutes

COOKING TIME: 40-45 minutes

OVEN TEMPERATURE: 325°F

MAKES: 1 cake, 8 inches in
diameter

¾ cup butter or margarine
¾ cup fine sugar
4oz semi-sweet chocolate, melted
¼ cup ground almonds
4 eggs, separated
½ cup regular flour
1 tsp baking powder
3 tblsp cornstarch

Frosting

2½ tblsp cocoa powder
2½ tblsp hot water
6 tblsp butter or margarine
1½ cups icing sugar

To Decorate

½ cup chopped toasted almonds
16 whole almonds, half dipped in
*   melted chocolate*

Grease and line two 8 inch cake pans. Cream the butter and sugar together until light and fluffy. Beat together the melted chocolate, ground almonds, and egg yolks, and add to the butter and sugar mixture. Fold the flour and cornflour into the mixture. Beat

the egg whites until stiff but not dry; fold into the cake mixture. Divide the mixture between the two pans. Bake in the oven for 40-45 minutes. Turn out and cool on a wire rack. To make the frosting: blend the cocoa powder with the hot water. Beat together the butter and confectioner's sugar until well mixed. Mix in the cocoa mixture. Use two-thirds of the frosting to sandwich the cakes together and cover the sides. Put the toasted nuts on a sheet of wax paper and roll the sides of the sandwiched cakes over the nuts. Smooth the remaining frosting over the top of the cake. Decorate with the whole almonds, half dipped in melted chocolate.

This page: Humpty Dumpty (top) and Moon Cake (bottom)

Facing page: Raspberry Torte (top) and Austrian Sachertorte (bottom).

saucepan with the brandy and bring just to the boil. Add the grated dark semi-sweet chocolate and stir until thick and smooth. Pour the chocolate mixture evenly over the cake and leave it to set. Melt the milk chocolate and place in a wax pastry bag fitted with a plain "writing" tip. Write "Sachertorte" across the top. Dust with confectioner's sugar if liked.

Chocolate Raspberry Torte

PREPARATION TIME: 45 minutes
COOKING TIME: 35-40 minutes
OVEN TEMPERATURE: 325°F
MAKES: 1 cake, 12 inches in diameter

1 recipe Family Chocolate Cake mixture (see recipe)
⅓ cup rum or Framboise
6 tblsp raspberry jam
1lb fresh raspberries
Bittersweet Butter Cream (see recipe)
20 chocolate leaves (see recipe)

Chocolate Frosting
2 tsp oil
2 tblsp butter
6oz semi-sweet chocolate, grated
1¼ tblsp Framboise or rum

Grease and flour a 12 inch deep pizza pan. Fill with the cake mixture. Bake until it springs up when pressed on top. Leave to cool in the pan for 5 minutes. Remove from the pan and let the cake cool on a wire rack for at least 2 hours. Slice the cake into two layers, horizontally, using a long knife. Sprinkle the cut surfaces with either the Framboise or rum. Spread one layer of the cake with raspberry jam and then with bittersweet butter cream; sandwich the cake back together again. Turn the cake upside down and chill. To make the frosting, put the oil and butter into a saucepan and stir constantly over a medium heat. Let the mixture simmer for a minute. Remove from the heat and add the chocolate and the Framboise or rum. Beat until the chocolate has

melted and the frosting is smooth. Let the frosting cool and spread the frosting over the top and sides of the cake. Put the raspberries on the top of the cake, in the middle, and put the chocolate leaves round the circle of raspberries. Refrigerate the cake for 1 hour. Note: this cake is best consumed on the day it is made.

Raspberry Torte

PREPARATION TIME: 25 minutes
COOKING TIME: 45 minutes
OVEN TEMPERATURE: 350°F
MAKES: 1 cake, 8 inches in diameter

4 eggs, separated
½ cup fine sugar
3 tblsp cocoa powder
¼ cup fresh white breadcrumbs
½ cup ground almonds

Filling
4 tblsp Raspberry jam
⅔ cup heavy cream, whipped

To Decorate
Fresh raspberries
Cocoa powder to dust

Grease and line an 8 inch round cake pan. Beat the egg yolks and sugar until thick and fluffy. Sieve the cocoa powder into the breadcrumbs. Fold into the egg yolks. Beat the egg whites in a large, dry bowl until they are fluffy and stiff. Fold half the egg whites into the cake mixture taking care not to deflate the meringue; fold in the almonds followed by the remaining egg whites. Put the mixture into the prepared cake pan. Bake in the oven for 45 minutes. Cool in the pan for a few minutes, and then turn onto a wire rack to cool. Split the cake in half horizontally. Spread one layer of the cake with the jam, and then with half the whipped cream. Decorate with the remaining cream on the top of the cake and garnish with raspberries. Dust the cake with cocoa powder.

Devil's Food Cake

PREPARATION TIME: 35 minutes
COOKING TIME: 1 hour 45 minutes-2 hours
OVEN TEMPERATURE: 300°F
MAKES: 1 cake, 8 inches in diameter

¾ cup butter or margarine
¾ cup soft brown sugar
2 eggs, beaten
¾ cup corn syrup
¼ cup ground almonds
1½ cups regular flour
6 tblsp cocoa powder
⅔ cup milk
¼ tsp bicarbonate of soda

American Frosting
1 egg white
1⅛ cups confectioner's sugar
1¼ tblsp corn syrup
3½ tblsp water
Pinch of salt
1 tsp lemon juice

To Decorate
Chocolate curls

Grease and line an 8 inch cake pan with wax paper. Cream the butter and sugar together until light and fluffy. Add the eggs gradually, beating well after each addition. Sieve together all the dry ingredients. Add the corn syrup and the milk to the creamed mixture. Fold in the dry ingredients and beat well with a wooden spoon. Pour the mixture into the prepared cake pan. Bake until a skewer inserted in the center comes out clean. Turn out and cool on a wire rack. To make the frosting: place all the frosting ingredients into a basin over a saucepan of hot water; beat until the frosting stands in peaks. Remove from the heat and continue beating until the mixture has cooled. Spread over the cake using a palette knife. (The frosting must be used as soon as it is made.) Decorate with the chocolate curls.

Truffle Torte (top) and Chocolate Raspberry Torte (right).

Humpty Dumpty

PREPARATION TIME: 50 minutes
COOKING TIME: 40-50 minutes
OVEN TEMPERATURE: 325°F
MAKES: 1 cake

1 cup butter or margarine
1 cup fine sugar
4 eggs, lightly beaten
1½ cups regular flour
1½ tsp baking powder
2½ tblsp cocoa powder
12oz Butter Frosting (see recipe)
Colored chocolate buttons
Liquorice strips
8oz marzipan

Grease a 1¼ pint pudding basin, and grease and line a 7 inch square shallow pan. Cream the butter and sugar together until light and fluffy. Beat in the eggs and then sieve the flour and baking powder into the mixture. Mix the cocoa powder with a little water to make a paste. Mix this into the cake mixture. Put two-thirds of the cake mixture into the pudding basin and the rest into the pan. Bake the pudding cake for 40-50 minutes, and the square cake for 30 minutes. Cool on a wire rack. To frost the cake: cut the square cake in half and then cut each half into 4 rectangles. Using the rectangles of cake as bricks, make a wall 2 bricks high and 4 across, sandwiching them together with butter frosting. Spread some of the remaining frosting on the top of the wall. Cover the pudding basin cake completely with butter frosting and put Humpty's eyes and nose on, using chocolate buttons. Use the liquorice to make a mouth.

Roll out the marzipan and shape legs and arms. Fix in position with cocktail sticks. You can even make a little hat by making a marzipan cup and pulling out a brim.

Chocolate Potato Cake

PREPARATION TIME: 55 minutes, plus cooling time

COOKING TIME: 30 minutes

OVEN TEMPERATURE: 375°F

MAKES: 1 two layer cake, 7 inches in diameter

½ cup hot mashed potato
2½ tblsp heavy cream
¾ cup + 2 tblsp sugar
2oz semi-sweet chocolate, melted
5 tblsp unsalted butter, softened
4 tsp bicarbonate of soda
2½ tblsp water
3 eggs, separated
1 cup flour
1 tsp baking powder
½ tsp rum
¼ cup milk
¼ tsp salt

Cocoa and Rum Frosting
3 tblsp unsalted butter
1¾ cups confectioner's sugar
2½ tblsp cocoa powder
¼ tsp salt
2 tsp rum
1½ tblsp strong black coffee

Butter and line two 7 inch round cake pans with wax paper. Brush the paper with a little melted butter and dust with flour. Mix the mashed potato and cream together in a bowl over a saucepan of hot water. Beat the softened butter and sugar together until soft and creamy. Add the potato and cream mixture to the butter and sugar and stir in the melted chocolate. Dissolve the bicarbonate of soda in the water and add to the mixture. Beat the egg yolks into the mixture one at a time. Sieve together the flour, baking powder and salt. Fold the flour into the mixture, adding the milk and rum alternately. Beat the egg whites until stiff but not dry. Gently fold in a third of the egg whites, and then fold in the remainder. Divide the mixture between the pans. Bake in a preheated oven for 30 minutes, or until a skewer inserted into the center comes out clean. Leave the cakes in the pans for 5 minutes before turning them out onto a wire rack to cool. For the frosting:

beat the butter until soft and creamy. Sieve together the confectioner's sugar, cocoa powder and salt; beat into the butter. Stir in the rum and coffee. Spread a layer of frosting on top of one cake and sandwich the cakes together; frost the top and sides of the cake with the remaining frosting.

Black Forest Gateau

PREPARATION TIME: 35 minutes

COOKING TIME: 55 minutes

OVEN TEMPERATURE: 325°F

MAKES: 1 cake, 7 inches in diameter

4oz semi-sweet chocolate, grated
1 cup regular flour
1¼ tsp baking powder
3 tblsp cornstarch
Generous pinch salt
10 tblsp butter, softened
½ cup fine sugar
4 eggs, separated
1¼ cups heavy cream, whipped
4 tblsp black cherry jam

To Decorate
4oz semi-sweet chocolate, grated

Grease and line a 7 inch round cake pan. Melt the chocolate in a basin over hot water. Sieve the flours and salt together. Cream the butter and sugar together until light and fluffy. Add the melted chocolate and egg yolks and beat well. Beat the egg whites until they are stiff and form peaks. Fold the egg whites lightly but thoroughly into the cake mixture. Spoon the mixture into the prepared cake

This page: Chocolate Mushroom Cake (top) and Chocolate Valentine Basket (bottom).

Facing page: Black Forest Gateau (top) and Devil's Food Cake (bottom).

pan. Bake in the oven for 55 minutes. Cool the cake in the pan and then turn it out onto a wire rack. Split the cake into two, horizontally. Spread one half with the jam and then with a third of

the cream; sandwich together with the remaining cake layer. Spread one half of the remaining cream over the top of the cake. Fit a large star tip to a pastry bag and fill with the remaining cream. Shape 8 rosettes on the top of the cake. Sprinkle the grated chocolate on the top of the cake. (You can top each rosette of cream with a black cherry, if liked.)

Chocolate Lemon Cake

PREPARATION TIME: 30 minutes
COOKING TIME: 40-45 minutes
OVEN TEMPERATURE: 350°F
MAKES: 1 2lb cake

¾ cup butter or margarine
¾ cup soft brown sugar
3 eggs
Grated rind of 1 lemon
2 cups regular flour
2 tsp baking powder
4oz semi-sweet chocolate, melted

Frosting
¾ cup butter
1lb confectioner's sugar, sieved
2½ tblsp lemon juice

To Decorate
Crystallized orange and lemon slices

Grease and line a 2lb rectangular pan or loaf pan. Cream the butter and sugar together until light and fluffy. Beat in the eggs, one at a time, adding a little sieved flour with each egg. Beat in the lemon rind and remaining flour, and then the chocolate. Pour into the prepared pan. Bake in the oven for 40-45 minutes. Turn onto a wire rack to cool. To make the frosting: put all the ingredients into a mixing bowl and beat together with a wooden spoon until well mixed. Cut the cake in half and use half the butter cream to sandwich the cake together. Spread the remaining frosting on the top of the cake and decorate with crystallized orange and lemon slices.

Chocolate Valentine Basket

PREPARATION TIME: 25 minutes
COOKING TIME: 40-45 minutes
OVEN TEMPERATURE: 325°F
MAKES: 1 heart-shaped cake

1 recipe Family Chocolate Cake mixture (see recipe)

Frosting
10 tblsp butter
1¼ cups confectioner's sugar
1¼ tblsp milk
2½ tblsp hot water
1¼ tblsp cocoa powder
Sweets for filling

Bake the Family Chocolate Cake mixture in two 8 inch heart-shaped cake pans for 40-45 minutes. Leave to cool on a wire rack. Cream the butter and the confectioner's sugar together with the milk. Mix the hot water and cocoa powder into a paste. Add this to the butter mixture and cream well. Fit two pastry bags with tips; one a ribbon tip, and the other a plain writing tip. Fill the bags with the butter cream. Hold the ribbon tip sideways and draw three evenly-spaced lines, one above the other, on one of the cakes. The three lines should all be the same length. Draw a vertical line, using the writing tube, along the edge of the basket weaving. Continue this process until the cake is covered. Cover the outermost edge and the sides of the remaining cake in the same way. This will now be the base, and the completely covered cake the lid. Arrange the lid at an angle on top of the lower cake and fill the inside with sweets.

Moon Cake

PREPARATION TIME: 20 minutes
COOKING TIME: 35 minutes
OVEN TEMPERATURE: 350°F
MAKES: 1 cake, 9 inches in diameter

This cake is fun to make and to eat. The mixture bubbles during baking and leaves a cake with a rocky, moon-like surface.

1¾ cups regular flour
½ cup granulated sugar
½ cup brown sugar
1 tsp salt
5 tblsp cocoa powder
6 tblsp melted butter
1 tsp vanilla essence
2½ tsp baking powder
1¼ tblsp white wine vinegar
⅔ cup milk
4oz marshmallows
Confectioner's sugar

Put the flour, sugar, salt and cocoa directly into a 9 inch cake pan and stir well until you have a light brown moon sand texture. Make a big crater in the middle of the sand so you can see the base of the pan, then a medium sized crater somewhere else in the sand, and a smaller crater on the other side (make sure that they are well apart). Spoon the baking powder into the medium sized crater. Spoon the melted butter into the large crater and the vanilla into the smallest crater. Now pour the vinegar into the medium sized crater and it will bubble and foam and become "volcanic". When this stops, pour the milk over the moon sand and stir well. The sand will now look like mud. Scatter the marshmallows over the surface. Bake for 35 minutes. (Test with a cocktail stick or skewer to see that the cake is done.) Dust with confectioner's sugar and serve from the pan.

Chocolate Mushroom Cake

PREPARATION TIME: 1 hour
COOKING TIME: 3 hours
OVEN TEMPERATURE: 225°F
MAKES: 1 cake, 9 inches in diameter

1 recipe Family Chocolate Cake mixture (see recipe)
Frosting recipe for Family Chocolate Cake
2oz white chocolate, melted
3 chocolate flakey bars
Confectioner's sugar

Meringue Mushrooms
2 egg whites
½ cup fine sugar
Oil for greasing
Cocoa powder
3oz dark semi-sweet chocolate, melted

Make the Family Chocolate Cake as instructed. Bake as directed and coat with frosting. Fill a pastry bag fitted with a small writing tip with the melted white chocolate. Make a spiral of melted white chocolate on top of the cake, working from the middle outwards. Cut the chocolate flakey bars in half, dust them with confectioner's sugar, and stick them around the sides of the cake to represent bark. To make the meringues: beat the egg whites in a bowl until they are stiff but not dry. Add the sugar slowly, beating well after each addition. Lightly oil a cooky sheet and cover with wax paper. Fit a pastry bag with a ½-¾ inch plain tip. Fill the bag with the meringue mixture. Pipe 12 mushroom stems on half the cooky sheet. Lift the bag vertically until the stems are 1½-2 inches high. Cut the meringue away from the tip. Then pipe 12 even rounds of meringue 1½-2 inches in diameter and 3-4 inches thick. (These make the mushroom tops; make sure that they are flat.) Sieve the cocoa powder over the meringues and then bake in a pre-heated oven until they are dried out (about 3 hours). Leave to cool. When the meringues are cool, spread melted chocolate on the underside of each mushroom top and fix the stem onto the chocolate. Leave to cool until the chocolate has set. Remove the mushrooms and stick a few of them on the cake, using a little more melted chocolate. Lay the others around the cake, to be eaten separately.

Chocolate Rolled Wafer Gateau

PREPARATION TIME: 40 minutes
COOKING TIME: 25-30 minutes
OVEN TEMPERATURE: 350°F
MAKES: 1 gateau, 8 inches in diameter

3 eggs
6 tblsp fine sugar
1½ tblsp cocoa powder
½ tsp baking powder
10 tblsp regular flour

Filling and Decoration
1¼ cups heavy cream
4oz packet English rolled wafers
1 oz semi-sweet chocolate, melted

Grease and line two 8 inch cake pans. Place the eggs and sugar in a basin and beat over a saucepan of hot water until thick and pale. Remove from the heat and beat until cool. Sieve together the coco powder, baking powder and flour, and gently fold into the mixture. Divide the mixture between the two prepared pans. Bake for 25-30 minutes. Turn out carefully onto a wire rack and cool. Whip the cream until thick and use a little to sandwich the cakes together. Spread a little cream around the sides and secure the English rolled wafers round the edge of the cake. Spread the remaining cream on the

of the cake. Put the melted
chocolate into a wax pastry bag
with a small hole, and drizzle over
cream; swirl it with a skewer.

Chocolate Rolled Wafer Gateau
(right) and Chocolate Lemon
Cake (below).

Truffle Torte

PREPARATION TIME: 1 hour

COOKING TIME: 1 hour 15 minutes

OVEN TEMPERATURE: 350°F

MAKES: 1 cake, 7 inches in diameter

½ cup unsalted butter, softened
½ cup fine sugar
3 eggs, separated
4oz semi-sweet chocolate, melted
¼ cup regular flour
10 tblsp finely ground hazelnuts

Chocolate Frosting

⅔ cup heavy cream
5oz semi-sweet chocolate, broken into pieces

Butter and line a 7 inch springform cake pan with wax paper. Brush the paper with a little melted butter and dust with flour. Beat the butter until soft and creamy. Add the sugar and continue to beat until light and fluffy. Add the egg yolks, one at a time, and beat well. Stir in the melted chocolate. Sieve together the flour and the ground hazelnuts and fold them into the cake mixture. Beat the egg whites until stiff but not dry. Gently fold in the beaten egg whites. Pour the mixture into the prepared pan. Bake in the pre-heated oven for about 1 hour. (When cooked the cake should be springy to the touch.) Remove from the oven and leave the cake in its pan for 5 minutes. Turn onto a wire rack and cool completely. To make the chocolate frosting: put the cream into a saucepan and bring to the boil. Add the chocolate, stirring until the chocolate has melted, and the mixture is thick and smooth. Pour the frosting evenly over the cake before it has a chance to set. Decorate with shaped chocolate whirls (see Cookies and Confections recipe).

Family Chocolate Cake

PREPARATION TIME: 25 minutes

COOKING TIME: 45-50 minutes

OVEN TEMPERATURE: 325°F

MAKES: 1 cake, 9 inches in diameter

1¾ cups regular flour
1 tsp bicarbonate of soda
1¼ tsp baking powder

2½ tblsp cocoa powder
10 tblsp soft brown sugar
2½ tblsp corn syrup
2 eggs
⅔ cup oil
⅔ cup milk

Frosting

6oz semi-sweet chocolate, chopped or grated
2½ tblsp light cream

To Decorate

Walnut halves

Grease and line a 9 inch cake pan. Sieve all the dry ingredients together in a large bowl. Put the sugar, syrup, eggs, oil and milk into a well in the center of the dry ingredients. Beat thoroughly until the mixture is smooth. Pour the mixture into the prepared cake pan. Bake for 45-50 minutes until a skewer inserted in the center of the cake comes out clean. Leave the baked cake in its pan for a few minutes and turn onto a wire rack to cool. To make the frosting: place the chocolate and cream into a small, heavy-based pan and heat gently until melted. Cool slightly and pour evenly over the cake. Decorate with walnuts.

Chocolate Cup Cakes

PREPARATION TIME: 20 minutes

COOKING TIME: 15 minutes

OVEN TEMPERATURE: 350°F

MAKES: 18

½ cup soft margarine
½ cup fine sugar
2 eggs
¾ cup regular flour
1 tsp baking powder
3 tblsp cocoa powder

Fudge Frosting

1 tblsp corn syrup
1lb granulated sugar
¼ cup unsalted butter
6 tblsp cocoa powder

Line 2 bun trays with 18 paper cake cases. Put all the cake ingredients into a bowl and beat together with a wooden spoon, until smooth and glossy. Put one small spoonful of the mixture into each of the cake cases. Bake in the center of the oven for 15 minutes or until they are firm to touch. To make the frosting: put the syrup into a saucepan with 1 cup cold water, the sugar, butter and cocoa powder; stir over a low heat until the sugar dissolves. Boil the mixture until a

little will form a soft ball when dropped into cold water. (Do not stir the mixture, just cut it with a wooden spoon occasionally.) Remove the mixture from the heat and allow it to cool for 10 minutes. Beat it with a wooden spoon until the mixture begins to thicken to a coating consistency. Pour the mixture over the cup cakes and allow it to set. (If the frosting sets before it has covered all the cakes, melt it gently.)

Spider's Web

PREPARATION TIME: 50 minutes

COOKING TIME: 35 minutes

OVEN TEMPERATURE: 375°F

MAKES: 1 cake, 7½ inches in diameter

1¼ cups regular flour
6 tblsp cocoa powder
½ tsp bicarbonate of soda
½ cup soft margarine
1 cup dark soft brown sugar
2 eggs
2 tsp peppermint essence
2 tblsp ground almonds
⅔ cup soured cream

To Decorate

4oz unsweetened chocolate, grated
1⅛ cups confectioner's sugar
1 dark chocolate button
Green food coloring
Peppermint essence
1 cup Butter Frosting (see recipe)
1 liquorice shoe-lace
1 chocolate-covered marshmallow
1 packet white chocolate buttons

Grease and line two 7½ inch cake pans. Sieve the flour, cocoa powder and bicarbonate of soda into a bowl and then add all the other ingredients. Mix well until they are blended. Divide the mixture between the two pans. Slightly hollow out the centers so that the

This page: Chocolate Cup Cakes (top) and Family Chocolate Cake – shown with candy covered chocolate sweets – (bottom).

Facing page: Nouvelle – Truffle Cake (top) and Sherry Cream Pie (bottom).

tops will be flat when baked. Bake in the oven for 35 minutes, until a wooden skewer inserted through the center comes out clean. Cool the cakes slightly in their pans and then turn onto a wire rack. Melt half the chocolate in a bowl over a pan of simmering water. Mix the sieved confectioner's sugar with a few drops of water to give a coating consistency. Put the melted chocolate into a pastry bag fitted with a small, plain tip. Cover the top of one of the cakes with the white frosting. Immediately shape a spiral of chocolate onto the white frosted cake, working outwards from the center. To make the web, mark out 12 lines by drawing a skewer across the frosting, from the center outwards. Put the dark chocolate drop in the center and leave to set. Add a little green coloring and peppermint essence to the butter frosting. Spread some of the green peppermint butter frosting over the un-frosted cake and place the frosted cake on top. Spread some of the remaining green frosting around the sides of the cake. Sprinkle the remaining grated chocolate around the sides of the cake. To make the spider: cut the liquorice into 8 equal lengths. Stick each length into the side of the chocolate marshmallow and trim the two front legs, making them a little shorter than the others. Using a little frosting, stick two white buttons on the front of the marshmallow for eyes. Put small liquorice trimmings onto the white chocolate drops, fixing them in place with a little more frosting. Place the spider on the cake.

Birthday Salute
Tanks

PREPARATION TIME:	45 minutes
COOKING TIME:	25 minutes
OVEN TEMPERATURE:	375°F

1 recipe Family Chocolate Cake mixture (see recipe)
12oz Chocolate Butter Frosting (see recipe)
1 packet chocolate chips
6 chocolate flakey bars

Grease and line a 7 inch square cake pan. Fill the pan with the family chocolate cake mixture and spread evenly in the pan. Bake as instructed, then leave to cool on a wire rack. Cut the cake in half. Cut off a piece from each half, measuring 2x2 inches. Cover the larger cake pieces with butter icing.

Spider's Web (above) and Birthday Salute (right).

Put the smaller pieces of cake on top of the larger pieces of cake, slightly towards the back. Stick 5 chocolate chips along both of the longer sides of each lower cake. Then put one chip on top for the hatch lid. Reserve two chocolate flakey bars, then cut the rest into short lengths. Lay the short lengths as tracks around the outer edges of the cakes. Push the whole flakey bars into the front of the smaller cakes to make the gun barrels.

Cannon

PREPARATION TIME: 10 minutes
COOKING TIME: 12 minutes
OVEN TEMPERATURE: 400°F

3 eggs
6 tblsp fine sugar
Vanilla essence
¾ cup regular flour
3 tblsp cocoa powder
1½ tblsp warm water

1 recipe Chocolate Butter Frosting

To Decorate
Confectioner's sugar
4 large chocolate flakey bars
Chocolate balls

Grease and line a 9 inch jelly roll pan. Beat the eggs, sugar, and a few drops of vanilla essence in a bowl over a pan of hot water until pale and thick (use an electric beater if possible). Sieve together the flour and cocoa powder, and then fold into the egg mixture with the water. Turn the mixture into the prepared pan and spread evenly. Bake for 12 minutes until the cake has risen. Sprinkle some confectioner's sugar onto a sheet of wax paper and turn the cake out onto the paper. Peel off the lining paper which may be stuck to the cake, and trim off any crisp edges that may be around the cake. Lay a piece of wax paper over the top of the cake and roll up the cake with the wax paper inside. Leave to cool on a wire rack. Unroll the cake and remove the paper. Spread with some of the butter frosting and re-roll. Dust the cake with confectioner's sugar. To decorate: fit a star tip onto a pastry bag and fill with some of the butter cream. Cut the jelly roll into 12 pieces, then cut 4 of the slices in half. Place two halves side by side, standing them on their flat edges. With a dab of butter cream, attach two whole slices on each of the sides. Make stripes of butter frosting down the middle of each cannon and lay the flakey bar on it, angled up at one end. Next to the cannon place a pile of chocolate balls, to represent cannon balls.

Chocolate Nut Gateau

PREPARATION TIME: 30 minutes, plus chilling

MAKES: 1 gateau, 7 inches in diameter

2 tblsp butter
1 tblsp corn syrup
1½ cups crunchy breakfast cereal

Filling
4½ tblsp cornstarch
1¼ tblsp cocoa powder
1¾ cups milk
⅔ cup chocolate flavored yogurt
1½ tblsp hazelnuts, skinned and roughly chopped

Topping
⅔ cup hazelnut-flavored yogurt
6 tblsp heavy cream, whipped

To Decorate
Grated chocolate
8 whole hazelnuts

Melt the butter and syrup in a saucepan. Add the crunchy cereal and mix well until they are coated with the butter syrup. Press the mixture into the base of a 7 inch fluted flan ring placed on a serving plate. Leave to cool. For the filling: mix the cornstarch and cocoa powder with a little of the milk. Heat the remaining milk until boiling and pour onto the cornstarch mixture, stirring constantly. Return the mixture to the pan and return to the heat; simmer for a few minutes, until thickened. Remove the saucepan from the heat and stir in the chocolate yogurt and chopped hazelnuts. Pour the mixture over the crisp base. For the topping: mix the nut yogurt with the whipped cream and spread it over the chocolate mixture. Put the flan in the refrigerator and chill until set. Carefully remove the flan ring and decorate with grated chocolate and whole hazelnuts. Serve with chocolate sauce if desired.

Chocolate Pistachio Loaf

PREPARATION TIME: 20 minutes

COOKING TIME: 1 hour 15 minutes-1 hour 30 minutes

OVEN TEMPERATURE: 350°F

MAKES: One 1lb loaf

1 cup regular flour
1¼ tsp baking powder
½ cup butter or margarine, softened
¼ cup fine sugar
2oz semi-sweet chocolate, chopped
½ cup pistachio nuts, chopped
2 tblsp ground almonds
2 eggs
2½ tblsp milk

Frosting
6oz semi-sweet chocolate, chopped or grated
A knob of butter

To Decorate
A few pistachio nuts, chopped

Grease and line a 1lb loaf pan. Put all the cake ingredients into a mixing bowl and beat until they are well mixed. Pour the mixture into the prepared pan. Bake in a pre-heated oven for 1 hour 15 minutes, or until cooked. Turn the cake out of the pan and leave to cool on a wire rack. For the frosting: melt the chocolate in a basin over a pan of hot water; beat the knob of butter

(the size of a walnut) into the chocolate and pour evenly over the cake. Sprinkle with chopped pistachio nuts.

Chocolate Knitting

PREPARATION TIME: 45 minutes

COOKING TIME: 40-45 minutes

OVEN TEMPERATURE: 325°F

MAKES: 1 cake, 9 inches square

1 recipe Family Chocolate Cake mixture (see recipe)
Butter frosting (see recipe)
2 tsp cocoa powder
1 packet of sugar strand cake decorations
2 large wooden knitting needles
10 chocolate flakey bars
10 inch square cake board

Bake the family chocolate cake mixture in a 9 inch square cake pan as directed. Cut the cake in half and sandwich the two halves together using some of the butter frosting. Put on the cake board. Mix the cocoa powder with 2 tsp boiling water and add this to the remaining butter frosting. Mix until smooth. Then add an extra 1¼ tblsp confectioner's sugar to the frosting so it will work better. Spread some of this frosting over the top of the cake. With a

warmed knife, cut 4 flakey bars in half and arrange them along the edge of the cake. Cut 4 flakey bars into quarters and place them with two pieces alternately, vertically and horizontally. Then cut two flakes into eight and repeat this process. Put the knitting needles into the cake; one goes on top, and the other goes through the center filling, so that the handles cross. Use the remaining frosting to fill a pastry bag fitted with a star tip. Make sticks of frosting over the top needle. Sprinkle the sugar strands over the top of the cake in a flaked pattern.

Dart Board

PREPARATION TIME: 45 minutes

COOKING TIME: 35 minutes

OVEN TEMPERATURE: 325°F

MAKES: 1 cake, 10 inches in diameter

1 cup butter
¾ cup soft light brown sugar
4 eggs
¾ cup corn syrup
3 tblsp cocoa powder
2 cups regular flour
2 tsp baking powder
1 tsp mixed ground spice
½ tsp ground ginger

To Decorate
12 inch cake board
4 tblsp apricot jam
12oz Butter Frosting (see recipe)
Generous pinch ground ginger
Grated chocolate
1 liquorice wheel
Small darts

Grease and line two 10 inch round cake pans. Cream the butter and sugar together; beat in the eggs slowly, followed by the corn syrup. Mix the cocoa powder with a few drops of water and make into a paste. Fold the flour into the cake mixture and then divide the mixture into two. Add the cocoa paste to one portion; sieve the mixed spice and ground ginger into the other portion, and add a little milk if necessary. Spread the two mixtures into their separate pans and hollow out the centers so the cakes will have a flat top when cooked. Bake in a pre-heated oven for 35 minutes. Leave to cool upside down on a wire rack, removing the paper. Put a 7 inch

ound plate on each cake and, using it as a guide, cut out a circle from the middle of each cake. Remove the circles and cut them into 20 even wedges. Put the ginger outer circle on the cake board and put the wedge slices – alternating between chocolate and ginger – in a circular pattern in the center. Spread the top of the cake with am and lay the chocolate ring on op of the ginger ring. Then repeat he process with the remaining

wedges, reversing the colors to get a chequered effect. Beat the butter frosting with the ginger and spread some of it around the sides of the cake. Cover the sides of the cake with grated chocolate. Fill a pastry bag fitted with a plain writing tip with butter frosting. Write the numbers on the cake in the correct order. Fit a star tip to the pastry bag, refill with the remaining butter icing, and shape shells for the scoring circles. Make a line around

the top and bottom of the outer edges and stick the liquorice wheel in the center for the bullseye. Put on the darts for decoration.

Facing page: Chocolate Knitting (top) and Dart Board (bottom).

This page: Chocolate Pistachio Loaf (top) and Chocolate Nut Gateau (bottom).

Desserts and Pastries

Chocolate Pear Pie

PREPARATION TIME: 25 minutes, plus chilling

SERVES: 4-6 people

6 tblsp butter
8oz semi-sweet chocolate graham crackers, crushed
14½oz can of pear halves
2½ tsp arrowroot

To Decorate
Grated chocolate

Melt the butter in a saucepan and mix with the crushed biscuits. Press the crumb mixture into the base and up the sides of an 7 inch loose-bottomed, fluted quiche pan. Place in the refrigerator to set. Carefully remove the crumb case from the quiche pan; leave it on the base as this will make serving easier. Drain the juice from the pears and reserve. Arrange the pear halves in the pie case. Mix the arrowroot with half of the pear juice in a small saucepan and bring to the boil. Stir gently until the mixture thickens and clears. Cool slightly and then spoon over the pears. Chill briefly. Sprinkle with grated chocolate and serve with cream.

Chocolate Orange Pudding

PREPARATION TIME: 25 minutes

COOKING TIME: about 1¾ hours

SERVES: 4-6 people

1 recipe Steamed Chocolate Pudding mixture (see recipe)
2 oranges

Make the chocolate pudding mixture as directed. Finely grate the rind of 1 orange and add this to the mixture. Thinly slice the second orange and press the orange circles around the inside of a greased 2½ pint pudding basin; put one orange slice in the base. Fill with the pudding mixture. Cover and steam the pudding for about 1¾ hours. Serve with orange or chocolate sauce.

Chocolate Mousse

PREPARATION TIME: 20 minutes, plus chilling time

SERVES: 4-6 people

4oz semi-sweet chocolate, grated
2½ tblsp water
1¼ tblsp instant coffee
4 egg whites
½ cup sugar

To Decorate
A little reserved chocolate

Put most of the chocolate, and the water and coffee into a bowl; stand it over a pan of hot water. Stir the mixture occasionally until the

This page: Chocolate Brandy Cheesecake (top left), Chocola[te] Orange Pudding (top right) an[d] Chocolate Pear Pie (bottom)

Facing page: Chocolate Eclairs (top) and Chocolate Strudel (bottom).

chocolate has melted and the mixture is smooth. Beat the egg whites until stiff but not dry, gradually beating in half the sugar. Mix the remaining sugar into the chocolate mixture and fold in the meringue. Divide the mixture among 4-6 glasses and sprinkle with remaining grated chocolate. Chill briefly.

Strawberry Box

PREPARATION TIME: 50 minutes, plus chilling
SERVES: 6 people

Chocolate Case
8oz semi-sweet chocolate, chopped or grated
1 tblsp vegetable oil

Filling
6oz semi-sweet chocolate, chopped or grated
1¼ tblsp kirsch
2 egg yolks
⅔ cup heavy cream
⅔ cup light cream

Topping
8oz strawberries, hulled and halved
4 tblsp strawberry jam, sieved
1¼ tblsp kirsch
1oz unsweetened chocolate, chopped or grated
⅔ cup heavy cream

Line either a 6 inch square cake pan or an 7 inch round cake pan with a double thickness of foil. (Make sure that the foil comes above the top of the pan to make removal of the set chocolate case easy.) For the chocolate case: melt the chocolate with the vegetable oil; pour two-thirds into the prepared pan and turn and tilt the pan so that the sides and base are coated evenly. Allow the chocolate to set slightly and then repeat the process with the remaining melted chocolate. Leave it in a cool place until the chocolate has set completely. Remove the chocolate case from the pan by pulling the foil lining gently; peel the foil away carefully from the chocolate case. To make the filling: melt the chocolate. Remove from the heat and beat the kirsch and the egg yolks into the chocolate. Whip the heavy and light creams together until thick and then fold into the chocolate. Pour the chocolate cream into the prepared chocolate case. Chill until set. Arrange the strawberries on the top of the filled case. Bring the jam and the kirsch to the boil together and remove from the heat; allow to cool slightly. Spoon the topping glaze over the strawberries, but do not allow the

hot jam to run to the edge of the chocolate case or it will melt. The glaze will set in about 5 minutes. Melt the chocolate and allow it to cool. Whip the heavy cream until thick and beat in the chocolate. Shape the chocolate mixture decoratively around the case using a pastry bag.

Chocolate Eclairs

PREPARATION TIME: 20 minutes
COOKING TIME: 20-25 minutes
OVEN TEMPERATURE: 425°F
MAKES: 10-12

¼ cup butter or margarine
⅔ cup water
10 tblsp regular flour, sieved
2 eggs, beaten
⅔ cup heavy cream, whipped

Frosting
4oz semi-sweet chocolate, chopped or grated
1 tblsp butter

Melt the butter (or margarine) in a saucepan over a gentle heat. Add the water and bring it just to the boil. Remove the pan from the heat and add the flour. Beat the mixture well until it leaves the sides of the pan clean. Cool the mixture slightly, and beat in the eggs gradually, beating between each addition. Spoon the mixture into a pastry bag fitted with a ½ inch plain tip. Make 3 inch lengths onto a lightly dampened cooky sheet. Bake in a preheated oven for 20-25 minutes until crisp and golden brown. Make a slit in the side of each eclair to allow the steam to escape, and cool on a wire rack. Fit a pastry bag with a ½ inch plain tip and spoon the whipped cream into the bag. Push the cream into each of the eclairs. Melt the chocolate and butter on a plate over a pan of hot water, stirring until smooth. Dip each eclair into the chocolate to give an even top coating and place on a wire rack to set.

Chocolate Strudel

PREPARATION TIME: 1 hour 30 minutes
COOKING TIME: 40 minutes
OVEN TEMPERATURE: 375°F
MAKES: a 14 inch strudel

1 cup regular flour
½ a beaten egg
½ tsp salt
⅓ cup water

A few drops of vinegar
6 tblsp butter, melted and cooled

Filling
3 tblsp butter
¼ cup vanilla sugar
2 eggs, separated
⅓ cup raisins
⅓ cup heavy cream
A pinch of ground cinnamon
2 tblsp fine sugar
2oz semi-sweet chocolate, grated
2½oz chopped walnuts
Confectioner's sugar

Sieve the flour into a large mixing bowl and make a well in the center. Beat together the egg, salt, water, vinegar and 1¼ tblsp of the melted butter. Pour this mixture into the well. Mix all the ingredients together to a dough. Knead the dough on a well-floured board until smooth and elastic (this will take about 15 minutes). Put the dough into a floured bowl and cover with a cloth. Leave for 15 minutes. While the dough is resting make the filling. Beat together the butter and vanilla sugar until light and fluffy. Add the egg yolks one at a time, beating after each addition. Add the walnuts, cream, cinnamon, chocolate and raisins and mix well. Beat the egg whites until stiff but not dry, and then gradually beat in the fine sugar. Fold this mixture gently into the

chocolate mixture. Cover the work surface with a large, clean cloth and dust the cloth with flour. Put the dough into the middle of the cloth and brush the tp with melted butter. Working around the dough, roll it out to a thickness of ⅛ inch. Brush it with more butter and, using four hands (you'll need to enlist help!), stretch the dough outwards as thinly as possible. Try to work around the dough so it does not tear. Cut the dough into a rectangle measuring 14x18 inches. Butter a large cooky sheet. Spoon the filling onto the strudel pastry, leaving a margin of 2 inches around three of the edges. Fold the margins over the filling and brush the remaining pastry with the melted butter. Gently lift the cloth so that the dough rolls itself up. Roll the dough onto the prepared cooky sheet. Bake for 40 minutes, basting with melted butter once or twice, until golden and crisp. Remove the strudel from the oven and dust with confectioner's sugar. Serve warm or cold. (Do not be put off by the thought of handling strudel pastry. Although a professionally thin pastry is needed for good results, it is not as difficult to achieve as its reputation would suggest.)

Strawberry Box (top right) and Chocolate Mousse (right).

Chiffon Pie

PREPARATION TIME: 40 minutes, plus chilling	
COOKING TIME: 1 hour	
OVEN TEMPERATURE: 375°F	
MAKES: 1 pie, 9 inches in diameter	

Shortcrust Pastry
2 cups regular flour
2 tblsp fine sugar
1 tsp salt
¼ cup ground almonds
10 tblsp unsalted butter, cut into pieces
1 egg yolk

Filling
1 cup milk
9 tblsp fine sugar
7oz unsweetened chocolate, broken into pieces
2 eggs, separated
1¼ tblsp powdered gelatin
4 tblsp strong black coffee
1½ cups heavy cream, whipped

Topping
1 cup heavy cream, whipped
Grated chocolate

To make the pastry: sieve the flour, sugar and salt and add the almonds. Make a well in the center of the dry ingredients and add the butter and egg yolk. Working quickly, use the fingertips to mix all the ingredients together. Shape the dough into a ball and wrap in foil or plastic wrap. Leave to chill for 1 hour. Roll out the pastry on a floured work surface to a thickness of ⅛-¼ inch and use to line a 9 inch fluted deep pie pan. Cover the pastry with a sheet of wax paper and weight it down with rice or beans. Bake blind in a pre-heated oven for 15 minutes, or until the edges begin to color. Remove the paper and beans and bake for a further 15 minutes. Leave to cool on a wire rack before removing from the pan. To make the filling: mix the milk, 6 tblsp of the sugar and the chocolate pieces in a saucepan; cook over a moderate heat. Stir constantly until the chocolate melts. The chocolate mixture should be thick and smooth when removed from the heat. Leave to cool. Beat the egg yolks into the chocolate mixture. Dissolve the gelatin in the coffee, over a low heat, and stir into the warm chocolate mixture. Chill until it begins to set. Beat the egg whites until stiff but not dry. Beat the remaining sugar into the beaten egg whites until stiff and glossy.

Gently fold the egg whites into the chocolate mixture, followed by the whipped cream. Pour the mixture into the pie shell. Decorate with whipped cream and grated chocolate.

Chocolate Terrine with Cherry Sauce

PREPARATION TIME: 40 minutes, plus freezing	
COOKING TIME: about 8 minutes	
MAKES: 1 3lb terrine	

8oz unsweetened chocolate, chopped or grated
1 cup unsalted butter
½ cup fine white sugar
⅓ cup confectioner's sugar
⅓ cup cocoa powder
½ cup granulated sugar
⅔ cup water
4 egg yolks, beaten
1⅓ cups heavy cream
4oz pitted black cherries

Sauce
2½ tblsp cornstarch

1¼ cups water
1lb pitted black cherries
½ cup granulated sugar
5 tblsp kirsch

Grease a 3lb loaf pan, and line with greased wax paper. Melt the chocolate in a bowl over a pan of hot water; remove from the heat and cool. Cream the butter and fine sugar until light and fluffy. Sieve the confectioner's sugar and cocoa together and beat into the butter mixture; beat in the cooled melted chocolate. Put the granulated sugar and water into a small, heavy-based pan and stir over a gentle heat until the sugar has dissolved. Boil quickly to 225°F on a sugar thermometer. Beat the egg yolks in a basin and add the sugar syrup; beat into a mousse-like consistency. Beat into the butter and chocolate mixture. Whip the cream and lightly fold it into the mixture. Fold in the pitted cherries and turn the mixture into the prepared pan. Freeze for 6 hours or until firm.

Cherry Sauce
Blend the cornstarch with 3 tblsp water in a small bowl. Put the cherries into a pan with the

remaining water and sugar and bring to the boil. Remove the pan from the heat and stir in the cornstarch mixture. Bring back to the boil, stirring continuously. Remove from the heat and add the kirsch. Serve the Chocolate Terrine in slices, accompanied by the hot cherry sauce.

Banana and Chocolate Trifle

PREPARATION TIME: 30 minutes	
SERVES: 6 people	

1 packet pineapple jelly
3 bananas
1 chocolate jelly roll
1¼ tblsp cornstarch
2½ tblsp fine sugar
2½ cups milk
2½ tblsp cocoa powder
⅔ cup heavy cream

To Decorate
4 glace cherries

Make up the jelly following the instructions on the packet. As the jelly is about to set, slice two bananas and stir them into the jelly. Pour into a pretty glass dish. When the jelly has cooled (but not set), cut the jelly roll into eight pieces and arrange the slices around the sides of the dish, standing up in the jelly. Mix the cornstarch and the sugar with a little of the milk; add the cocoa powder and mix well. Add the remaining milk. Put the chocolate mixture into a small saucepan and boil for a few minutes, stirring until it thickens. Leave to cool. Lightly whip the cream and fold into the cold custard. Pour the mixture into the dish on top of the jelly. Before serving, decorate the top of the trifle with slices of the remaining banana and the glace cherries.

This page: Chocolate Terrine with Cherry Sauce (top) and Tarte au Chocolat (bottom).

Facing page: Banana and Chocolate Trifle (top) and Chiffon Pie (bottom).

Chocolate Rum Fool

PREPARATION TIME: 20 minutes, plus chilling

SERVES: 4-6 people

⅔ cup raisins
5 tblsp dark rum
1 cup cold cooked potato
¼ cup sugar
7oz semi-sweet chocolate cake covering
1 cup butter
⅔ cup heavy cream

Soak the raisins in the rum for one hour. Sieve the potato and beat in the rum-soaked raisins and the sugar. Melt the chocolate and the butter together. Remove from the heat and beat into the potato mixture. Whip the cream until thick, and gently fold two-thirds of it into the mixture. Turn the mixture into a serving dish and chill in the refrigerator for at least one hour. Decorate with the remaining cream when ready to serve.

Chocolate and Cherry Mousse

PREPARATION TIME: 35-40 minutes, plus chilling

SERVES: 6 people

Cherry Mousse
12oz pitted cherries, fresh or canned
1½ tsp gelatin powder
2½ tblsp cold water
¼ cup sugar
2 eggs, separated
⅔ cup heavy cream

Chocolate Mousse
6oz semi-sweet chocolate, chopped or grated
2 tsp instant coffee
1 tblsp water
4 eggs, separated
⅔ cup heavy cream

To Decorate
⅔ cup whipped cream
A few whole cherries

Rub the cherries through a sieve, or puree them in a blender or food processor. Sprinkle the gelatin over the cold water and leave in a basin to soften for a few minutes; dissolve the gelatin over a pan of simmering water. Remove from the heat and cool. Beat the sugar and egg yolks together until thick and creamy and then beat in the gelatin; stir in the cherry puree and mix well. Beat the egg whites in a dry bowl until stiff but not dry. Whip the cream lightly until it

holds its shape and then fold the cream gently into the cherry mixture. Fold the egg whites into the cherry mixture lightly but thoroughly. Pour into 6 individual serving dishes and chill for 30 minutes. For the chocolate mousse: melt the chocolate with the coffee and the water. Remove from the heat and beat in the egg yolks. Whip the cream lightly until it holds its shape, then beat the egg whites in a separate bowl until stiff but not dry. Fold the cream into the chocolate mixture and then the egg whites. Pour the chocolate mousse over the chilled cherry mousse and chill for at least an hour. Decorate with whipped cream and cherries before serving.

Chocolate Quiche

PREPARATION TIME: 30 minutes, plus chilling time

COOKING TIME: about 1 hour

OVEN TEMPERATURE: 375°F and then 350°F

SERVES: 10 people

1 cup regular flour
1¼ tsp baking powder
Pinch of salt
½ cup ground almonds
10 tblsp butter
1 egg yolk
Cold water

Filling
1lb 2oz cooking chocolate, grated
3 cups heavy cream
7 egg yolks

Mix the flour, salt and almonds in a bowl. Add the butter in small pieces and rub into a crumb-like texture. Beat the egg yolk with 2½ tblsp of water. Add to the crumble mixture and mix to a firm dough, adding a little extra water if required. Shape the dough into a ball; wrap and chill in the refrigerator. Flour a pastry slab or work surface and roll out the dough; use to line a large loose-bottomed quiche pan, 12 inches in diameter. Line the pastry with wax paper and beans and bake "blind" at the higher temperature for 10 minutes. Remove the paper and beans and bake for a further 3 minutes. Leave to cool. Melt the chocolate and cool slightly. Beat the cream and the egg yolks until they are well blended, and add the melted chocolate. Pour into the pastry case. Bake for 45 minutes at the lower temperature, until the top is firm to the touch. Allow the quiche to cool a little, and then serve in small portions with whipped cream and/or fruit.

Nouvelle – Truffle Cakes

PREPARATION TIME: 40 minutes

COOKING TIME: 18-20 minutes

OVEN TEMPERATURE: 375°F

MAKES 6

This is a very rich, sophisticated dessert, ideal for special occasions.

5 eggs, separated
3 tblsp granulated sugar
6 tblsp regular flour
3 tblsp cocoa powder
1 tsp baking powder
Pinch salt
2 tblsp melted unsalted butter
3oz semi-sweet chocolate, melted
Cocoa powder
Rum, Grand Marnier or Amaretto liqueur
⅔ cup heavy cream, well chilled
Frosting or vanilla sugar
1 recipe Nouvelle Chocolate Sauce (see recipe)
1 cup split almonds, lightly toasted and broken into pieces

To make the cake mixture: butter and flour six 4 inch individual souffle dishes. Line the base of each dish with buttered wax paper. Put the egg yolks and half the sugar into a bowl and beat well, preferably with an electric mixer, until the eggs are thick and pale. Sieve the flour, cocoa, baking powder and salt together. Beat the egg whites until stiff but not dry, gradually adding the remaining sugar. Fold the flour and melted butter alternately into the egg yolk mixture. Fold in the beaten egg whites lightly but thoroughly. Divide the mixture among the prepared dishes. Stand them on a cooky sheet and bake for 18-20 minutes, or until a skewer inserted in the center comes out clean. Take the cakes out of the oven and let them cool in their dishes. Remove them from their dishes, right way up, and cool on a wire rack. Trim the cakes a little so that they are rounded. Brush the tops and sides of the cakes with the melted chocolate and let it harden slightly before rolling them in the cocoa powder. Dig a little hole in the top of each cake. Sprinkle the inside of each cake with some of the liqueur you have chosen. About 30 minutes before serving, whip the cream until thick and flavor it with frosting or vanilla sugar and more of the chosen liqueur. Fit a pastry bag with a small rosette tip and fill with the cream. Fill the little hole in each cake with the cream and place the truffle cake hole-side down on

a small plate. Shape a small rosette of cream to decorate each cake. Mix the Nouvelle Sauce with the almonds: spoon it around the bottom of each cake, and a little over the top.

Chocolate and Cherry Mousse (right) and Chocolate Quiche (below).

Tarte au Chocolat

PREPARATION TIME: 25 minutes, plus chilling

COOKING TIME: 45 minutes

OVEN TEMPERATURE: 375°F

MAKES: 1 tart, 10 inches in diameter

2 cups regular flour
1 tsp salt
¼ cup ground almonds
2½ tblsp fine sugar
10 tblsp unsalted butter
1 egg yolk

Filling
1 cup heavy cream
2 tblsp brandy
7oz semi-sweet chocolate, chopped or grated
2 egg whites, beaten
¼ cup fine sugar

Topping
1¼ cups heavy cream
2 tblsp fine white sugar
Praline (see recipe) or grated chocolate

Grease and line a 10 inch quiche pan with wax paper. Sieve together the flour and salt and add the almonds and sugar; make a well in the center. Add the butter and egg yolk. Mix all the ingredients together, using the fingertips, to form a dough. Shape the dough into a ball and wrap in foil or plastic wrap. Chill for 1 hour. Roll the dough out on a floured work surface to about ⅛-¼ inch thick. Use the dough to line the prepared quiche pan. Cover with wax paper and weight it down with rice or beans. Bake "blind" for 10-15 minutes until it begins to turn pale golden. Remove the paper and beans and bake for a further 15 minutes. Leave the pastry case to cool in its pan. To make the filling: put the cream and brandy into a saucepan and bring just to the boil. Add the chocolate and stir until the mixture is thick and smooth. Leave to cool for at least 1 hour. Beat until fluffy. Beat the egg whites until stiff but not dry, adding the sugar slowly. Fold the meringue into the chocolate mixture. Remove the pastry case from its pan and fill it with the chocolate mixture. For the topping: beat the cream with the sugar until it is light and fluffy, and then spread it over the chocolate filling. Decorate with crushed praline or chocolate.

Chocolate Honeycomb

PREPARATION TIME: 20 minutes, plus chilling

SERVES: 4-6 people

½oz gelatin
3 eggs, separated
¼ cup sugar
1¾ cups milk
3oz semi-sweet chocolate, grated
Vanilla essence

Put the gelatin, sugar and egg yolks into a basin and beat until creamy. Heat the milk in a small saucepan; add the grated chocolate and stir until dissolved. Pour the chocolate milk over the beaten egg yolk and gelatin mixture; put the bowl over a pan of gently simmering water and stir continuously until the mixture is thick. Leave the mixture to cool. Add a few drops of vanilla essence to the thickened chocolate mixture. Beat the egg whites until stiff but not dry and fold in. Turn the mixture into a dampened mold and chill until set. Unmold carefully before serving.

Marbled Rum Cream Pie

PREPARATION TIME: 35 minutes, plus chilling

COOKING TIME: 10 minutes

SERVES: 6-8 people

1 cup sugar
A pinch of salt
5 tblsp water
1¼ tblsp gelatin
2 eggs, separated
¾ cup milk
5 tblsp dark rum
12oz semi-sweet chocolate, finely chopped
1 cup heavy cream
1 tsp vanilla essence
1 baked sweet shortcrust pastry pie case, 9 inches in diameter

Mix ¼ cup of the sugar with the salt, water and gelatin in a small, heatproof bowl; stand over a pan of simmering water and stir until the gelatin has dissolved. Remove the bowl from the heat and beat in the egg yolks, milk and rum. Return to the heat, and continue to beat until the mixture has thickened slightly. Remove from the heat and stir in

the chocolate until it has melted. Chill until thickened but not set. Beat the egg whites until stiff but not dry and gradually beat in ½ cup of the remaining sugar. Fold the meringue mixture into the chilled chocolate mixture. Whip the cream with the remaining sugar and vanilla essence until thick. Pile alternate spoons of cream and chocolate mixture into the cold cooked pastry pie case. Cut through the layers with a knife, to give a marbled effect. Chill well until firm.

Sherry Cream Pie

PREPARATION TIME: 30 minutes plus chilling time

COOKING TIME: 35 minutes

OVEN TEMPERATURE: 375°F

MAKES: 1 pie, 8 inches in diameter

1¼ cups flour
¼ cup sugar
⅓ cup butter
1 egg yolk

Filling
8oz semi-sweet dark chocolate, chopped or grated
4 tblsp medium sherry
1 tsp gelatin
4 eggs, separated

To Decorate
2oz semi-sweet chocolate, melted
⅔ cup heavy cream
1 tblsp sherry

Put the flour and the sugar into a bowl; add the butter, cut into small pieces, and the egg yolk. Knead to a smooth dough. Wrap the dough and chill for 30 minutes. Lightly flour the work surface and roll out the dough; use to line a 8 inch loose-bottomed pie pan. Prick the base of the pan with a fork. Line with wax paper and baking beans. Bake for 15 minutes; remove the paper and beans and bake for a further 15 minutes. Remove the pastry case from the pan and cool on a serving plate or platter. Put the chocolate into a small, heavy-based saucepan with the sherry and 2½ tblsp cold water. Sprinkle the gelatin over the top and stir over a low heat until the gelatin has dissolved. Beat the egg yolks into the sauce, one at a time, and cool the mixture. Whisk the egg whites until stiff but not dry and then fold it into the sauce. Pour the mixture into the prepared pastry case and

chill until set. Melt the chocolate. Lightly whip the heavy cream. Divide the cream in half; stir the sherry into one half, and the chocolate into the other. Fit two pastry bags with star tips and fill each bag with a different cream. Decorate the top of the pie with alternate stars of the different creams.

Steamed Chocolate Pud

PREPARATION TIME: 25 minutes
COOKING TIME: 1¾-2 hours
SERVES: 6 people

1 cup sugar
1 cup butter
4 eggs, beaten
1½ cups regular flour
6 tblsp cocoa powder
2½ tblsp rum

Butter a 2½ pint pudding basin. Beat the sugar and butter together until light and fluffy. Add the eggs gradually, beating well after each addition. Fold in the sieved flour, cocoa and the rum and mix well. Turn the mixture into the greased pudding basin. Cover the top with a double thickness of wax paper or foil, making a pleat in the top to give room for the pudding to rise. Tie round with string. Steam for 1¾-2 hours until well risen and spongy to the touch. Unmold the pudding and serve hot with a sauce of your choice.

Facing page: Marbled Rum Cream Pie (top) and Chocolate Honeycomb (bottom).

This page: Steamed Chocolate Pud (top) and Chocolate Rum Fool (bottom).

Fruits and Fantasies

Chocolate Dipped Pineapple with Melba Sauce

PREPARATION TIME: 40 minutes, plus chilling

SERVES: 6-8 people

1 good sized fresh pineapple
Rum
½ cup granulated sugar
1lb raspberries
6oz unsweetened chocolate, chopped or grated

Peel and slice the pineapple into rings, ½ inch thick. Sprinkle the slices first with the rum, and then with a little sugar. Cover and chill for at least one hour. Puree the raspberries and sieve them to remove the seeds. Sweeten with a little sugar to taste and add a little rum. Chill until needed. Melt the chocolate in a bowl over a saucepan of hot water. Remove the pineapple from the refrigerator and pat dry with absorbent paper. Cover a cooky sheet with waxed paper and partially dip each ring of pineapple into the melted chocolate. Leave on the waxed paper to harden (you can put them in the refrigerator). Put each pineapple ring onto an individual plate and pour a pool of melba sauce over just before serving.

Chocolate Souffle with Sour Cherries

PREPARATION TIME: 40 minutes

COOKING TIME: 10-12 minutes

OVEN TEMPERATURE: 400°F

SERVES: 6 people

½ cup sugar
3 eggs, separated
Vanilla essence
Grated rind of half a lemon
5 egg whites
1¼ tsp instant mashed potato powder
Melted butter for greasing
Sugar to dust
1¼ tsp arrowroot
13oz can sour cherries

Beat 2 tblsp of the sugar with the egg yolks, vanilla essence and lemon rind. Beat the egg whites with the remaining sugar until stiff but not dry; beat in the potato powder. Fold the snowy egg whites into the egg yolk mixture. Brush the surface of a metal serving dish with melted butter and sprinkle with a little sugar. Put ¾ of the souffle mixture into the dish with a spatula and smooth it out into a boat shape, hollowing out the middle. Fit a pastry bag with a star tip and fill with the remaining souffle mixture. Shape a border around the top and bottom of the boat. Bake in the oven for 10-12 minutes. Drain the canned cherries and keep the juice. Mix the juice with the arrowroot and stir over a low heat until it thickens. Add

This page: Locksmiths Lads (top) and Banana Fritters with Chocolate Rum Sauce (bottom).

Facing page: Chocolate Souffle with Sour Cherries (top) and Chocolate Dipped Pineapple with Melba Sauce (bottom).

most of the cherries. Fill the top of the souffle with the reserved cherries. Serve the cherry sauce separately. Note: the metal of the dish will conduct the heat evenly through the souffle.

Chocolate Waffles and Fruit Kebabs

PREPARATION TIME: 15 minutes

COOKING TIME: 15 minutes

SERVES: 4 people

2oz semi-sweet chocolate, chopped or grated
¼ cup water
⅓ cup unsalted butter
2 eggs
6-7 tblsp sugar
1½ cups regular flour
2½ tsp baking powder
½ cup milk
¾ cup chopped walnuts
Whipped cream or ice cream to serve

Stir the chocolate and water together in a small, heavy-based saucepan until the chocolate melts. Remove the pan from the heat when the chocolate forms a paste. Beat the butter into the melted chocolate, and then add the eggs and the sugar. Sieve the flour and baking powder onto a sheet of wax paper. Add the sieved flour and milk alternately to the chocolate mixture. Stir in the walnuts. Pour the batter into a hot, oiled waffle iron. Bring the cover down and cook for 2-3 minutes on either side. Serve with whipped cream, ice cream, and cocktail sticks threaded with pieces of fresh fruit.

Banana Fritters with Chocolate Rum Sauce

PREPARATION TIME: 20 minutes, plus standing time

COOKING TIME: 14-15 minutes

SERVES: 6 people

Almost any kind of fruit can be battered, and the accompanying sauces that can be used range from fruit purees to liqueured sauces, like the rum sauce in this recipe.

1¼ cups flour
⅔ cup white wine
2 eggs, separated
½oz drinking chocolate
1 tblsp sugar
6 bananas
Oil for deep frying
Confectioner's sugar for dusting

Sauce
A stick of butter
½ cup sugar
A pinch of salt
2½ tblsp dark rum
6 tblsp cocoa powder
⅔ cup heavy cream
1¼ tsp vanilla essence

Sieve the flour into a bowl and beat in the wine, egg yolks and drinking chocolate. Beat until smooth and let the batter stand for 15 minutes. Beat the egg whites and sugar until fluffy. Fold the fluffy egg whites into the batter. Slice the bananas into bite-sized pieces. Put each piece onto a fork and dip into the batter. Lower immediately into the hot oil, frying until the batter is golden brown. Lift out of the oil with a slotted spoon and leave to drain on a piece of absorbent paper. Dust with confectioner's sugar and serve with the sauce. To make the sauce: melt the butter in a small saucepan. Stir in the sugar, salt, rum and cocoa powder. Mix well over a low heat. Add the cream and bring to the boil. Simmer very gently for 5 minutes. Remove from the heat and add the vanilla essence. Note: you can use fresh butter to fry the fritters and this will give a very rich flavor, unlike lard or vegetable oil, which are usually well refined, and will not alter the natural flavor of the ingredients. The crisper the better, but be careful not to burn the fritters. You may have a tempura set which can be used when entertaining informally, or a thermostatically controlled deep fat fryer which will give you perfect results.

Locksmiths Lads
Beignets De Prunes Au Chocolat

PREPARATION TIME: 35 minutes

COOKING TIME: about 4 minutes

SERVES: 4 people

1¼ cups regular flour
2 eggs, separated
⅔ cup white wine
A pinch of salt
2½ tblsp cooking oil
2 tblsp sugar
16 large tenderized prunes
16 blanched almonds
Oil for deep frying
2oz grated chocolate
Confectioner's sugar to dust

Zabaione Sauce
3 egg yolks
1 whole egg
9 tblsp sugar
7½ tblsp marsala

Sieve the flour into a mixing bowl; make a well in the center and pour in the egg yolks, white wine, salt and the oil. Mix well using a wire whisk, and leave the batter to stand for 20 minutes. Beat the egg whites until stiff and fold in the sugar. Fold the egg whites into the batter. Carefully remove the stone from each prune and replace it with an almond. Spike the prunes with a fork and dip them into the batter. Fry the coated prunes in hot oil until they are golden brown; remove and drain them on absorbent paper. Scatter the grated chocolate over the prunes when they are nearly cold. Dust with confectioner's sugar. To make the sauce: cream the egg yolks, whole egg and sugar together in a heatproof bowl over a saucepan of simmering water. Add the marsala

to the mixture and beat it with a wire whisk until it doubles in volume, and is foamy. Serve immediately with the Locksmiths Lads.

Strawberry Shortcake

PREPARATION TIME: 15 minutes

COOKING TIME: 7-10 minutes

OVEN TEMPERATURE: 450°F

SERVES: 6 people

A wonderful dessert for the summer, with a luxurious topping.

2 cups regular flour
2½ tsp baking powder
¼ cup butter
2 tblsp sugar
1 egg, lightly beaten
Milk
12oz strawberries, hulled
1¼ cups heavy cream
1 recipe Chocolate Fudge Sauce (see recipe)

Chocolate Waffles and Fruit Kebabs (top right) and Strawberry Shortcake (right).

Sieve the flour and baking powder into a mixing bowl. Cut the butter into the mixture until it resembles breadcrumbs. Stir in the sugar. Add the beaten egg, and enough milk to bind the mixture into a stiff scone dough. Roll out the dough to a thickness of approximately ½ inch and cut out two circles. Put the circles of dough onto greased cooky sheets. Bake for 10 minutes (the shortcakes should be pale golden). Cool on a wire rack. Slice 8oz of the strawberries and whip the cream. Place one circle of the shortcake on a plate. Spoon half of the cream onto it and top with the sliced strawberries. Add a little more cream and place the second shortcake on top. Top the shortcake with spoonfuls of the remaining cream and the remaining strawberries. Drizzle over a little chocolate fudge sauce. Serve the remaining sauce separately.

Strawberry Fondue

PREPARATION TIME: 50 minutes

COOKING TIME: 20 minutes

SERVES: 6 people

Stand
*Oasis cone (from a florist) 12-15
    inches high*
Kitchen foil
Dress net
Ribbon bows

*2lb large strawberries, washed and
    hulled*
Cocktail sticks

Vanilla Fondue
12oz white chocolate, grated
⅓ cup evaporated milk
¼ tsp vanilla essence

Grand Marnier Fondue
6oz semi-sweet chocolate, grated
6oz sweet chocolate, grated
¾ + 2 tblsp cup heavy cream
2½ tblsp Grand Marnier

To make the stand: cover the oasis with kitchen foil and then cover it with the dress net (use a color that will go with the strawberries and with your table decoration). Place ribbon bows at random, fixing them into the oasis. Stick the strawberries into the stand, using cocktail sticks, so that they almost cover the cone completely. To make the vanilla fondue: melt the white chocolate with ⅔ of the evaporated milk in a pan over a low heat. Add the vanilla essence and then add the remaining evaporated milk as required. (The fondue should coat the back of a spoon.) To make the Grand Marnier fondue: melt together the chocolates and then add the cream. Stir well and remove from the heat. Finally add the liqueur. Pour the two fondues into separate warmed bowls. Keep these on a warming tray, or fondue tray, or on stands with night light candles beneath. Your guests can then pick strawberries and dip them into the fondues.

Chocolate Apricot Horns

PREPARATION TIME: 15 minutes

COOKING TIME: 15-20 minutes

OVEN TEMPERATURE: 425°F

MAKES: 10

8oz puff pastry
Beaten egg to glaze
4oz semi-sweet chocolate
1 tblsp butter
2½ tblsp brandy
¾ cup apricot puree
¾ cup heavy cream, whipped

To Decorate
Chocolate curls

Roll out the pastry into a rectangle about 10x13 inches and trim the edges. Cut into strips 1 inch wide. Dampen one long edge of each strip with water and wind round a metal cornet mold (start at the point and overlap the dampened edge as you go). Put the horns on a lightly dampened cooky sheet and chill for 15 minutes. Brush the horns with beaten egg and bake for 15-20 minutes until golden brown. Leave for 5 minutes, before carefully removing the molds; cool the pastry horns on a wire rack. Melt the chocolate with the butter on a plate, over a pan of hot water; dip each of the horns into the chocolate. Mix the brandy with the apricot puree and spoon a little into each of the horns. Fit a star tip to a pastry bag and fill the pastry bag with the whipped cream. Push the cream into the horns. Decorate with chocolate curls.

Profiteroles Vine

PREPARATION TIME: 30 minutes,
plus cooling

COOKING TIME: 25-30 minutes

OVEN TEMPERATURE: 400°F

SERVES: 4-6 people

Choux Pastry
⅔ cup water
¼ cup butter
10 tblsp flour, sieved
2 eggs, beaten

Filling
*1¼ cups cold chocolate vanilla sauce
    (English chocolate custard)*
⅔ cup heavy cream, whipped
6oz semi-sweet chocolate, melted
Chocolate Butter Sauce (see recipe)

For the pastry: heat the water and butter in a small saucepan until the butter melts. Bring to the boil; remove the pan from the heat and beat in the flour. Beat with a wooden spoon until it leaves the sides of the pan clean. Cool the mixture slightly, and gradually beat in the eggs, beating between each addition. (The mixture should be smooth and glossy.) Fill a pastry bag, fitted with a large, plain tip, with the choux pastry. Shape 20 even-sized balls onto two dampened cooky sheets. Bake in a pre-heated oven for 20-25 minutes, until well risen. Split each of the choux balls and let the steam escape; return to the oven for a further 2 minutes. To make the filling: follow a recipe for English custard and add 1¼ tblsp of cocoa. Stir the cream into the sauce, making sure that there are no lumps (beat if necessary). Fill a large pastry bag, fitted with a plain tip, with the cream sauce and fill the choux buns. To decorate and serve: coat a large leaf with melted chocolate; pipe a few curls and a stem onto a sheet of silicone paper. Leave them to set; gently peel off the paper and the leaf. Arrange the profiteroles to look like a bunch of grapes on a large serving tray or dish; add the chocolate leaf, stem and curls. Finally pour over the chocolate sauce.

**This page: Strawberry Fondue
(with Grand Marnier Fondue).**

**Facing page: Profiteroles Vine
(top) and Chocolate Apricot
Horns (bottom).**

Frozen Desserts

Mocha Ice Cream

PREPARATION TIME: 25 minutes, plus freezing

SERVES: 6 people

2½ tblsp instant coffee granules
¼ cup butter
½ cup soft brown sugar
5 tblsp cocoa powder
6 tblsp water
1¾ cups canned evaporated milk, chilled

Put the coffee, butter, sugar, cocoa and water into a saucepan, and heat gently. Stir the mixture until melted, and bring it to the boil. Cool. Beat the chilled evaporated milk in a bowl, until it is thick and frothy. Mix it into the cooled mixture, beating until it is well blended. Turn the mixture into a freezer container and freeze uncovered until slushy. Beat the ice cream well and re-freeze until firm.

Rum Ice Cream Gateau

PREPARATION TIME: 30 minutes, plus freezing

COOKING TIME: 1 hour

OVEN TEMPERATURE: 300°F

SERVES: 6-8 people

Oil for greasing
1 cup sugar
3 egg whites
1¼ tblsp instant coffee
2½ tblsp boiling water
1¾ cups heavy cream
2½ tblsp dark rum
⅔ cup chocolate ice cream

Lightly oil a baking sheet and line the base of a 7 inch round, loose-bottomed cake pan with greased wax paper. Beat ¼ cup of the sugar into the egg whites and continue to beat until stiff. Add the remaining sugar and beat until it peaks. Fill a pastry bag, fitted with a star tip, with the meringue mixture. Shape small rosettes onto the cooky sheet, keeping them well apart. Bake them in a pre-heated oven for 1 hour; leave in the oven for a further 20 minutes, with the oven turned off. Remove the meringues

from the oven and allow them to cool. Mix the coffee with the water in a small bowl. Beat the cream until thick; fold in all but 4 of the meringues. Add the coffee and the rum, taking care not to crush the meringues. Use the mixture to fill the prepared cake pan. Cover and freeze until firm. Soften the ice cream. When the gateau is hard enough, remove it from the pan.

Beat the ice cream and use it to fill a pastry bag fitted with a ½ inch star tip. Quickly shape rosettes on top of the gateau. Return the gateau to the freezer and leave until firm. Put the reserved meringues in the center of the gateau. Refrigerate for 10 minutes before serving.

This page: Mocha Ice Cream (top) and Rum Ice Cream Gateau (bottom).

Facing page: Chocolate Chip Ice Cream (top) and Chocolate Ice Box Cake (bottom).

Chocolate Ice Cream

PREPARATION TIME: 1 hour
40 minutes, plus freezing time

COOKING TIME: 15-20 minutes

SERVES: 8 people

4oz semi-sweet chocolate, chopped or
   grated
2½ cups milk
7 egg yolks
½ cup sugar

Put the chopped chocolate into a
saucepan with a little milk. Stir
over a low heat until the chocolate
melts and forms a smooth paste.
Add the remaining milk. Beat the
egg yolks and sugar together until
thick and light. Beat into the
chocolate milk. Beat continuously
over a low heat until thick. Pour
the mixture into a bowl and stand
over ice. (If you do not have a lot
of ice, chill in the refrigerator.)
Either pour into an ice cream
churn, and follow the manufacturer's instructions, or pour into ice
trays and freeze for 30 minutes. Tip
the par-frozen ice cream into a
bowl and beat until smooth.
Return to the freezer. Repeat this
process every 30 minutes, until the
ice cream is really thick. Freeze
until ready to serve.

Nougat Ice Cream Cake

PREPARATION TIME: 40 minutes,
plus freezing

SERVES: 6-8 people

¼ cup ground hazelnuts
16 small wafer biscuits
15½oz can pineapple chunks, or
8oz crystallised pineapple
1¾ cups vanilla ice cream
1¾ cups chocolate ice cream
4oz semi-sweet chocolate, finely
   chopped
4oz nougat
1¾ cups heavy cream, whipped

Grease a 1lb loaf pan and sprinkle
the inside with ground hazelnuts.
Put 12 of the wafer biscuits around
the sides and base of the pan.
Drain the pineapple chunks (or
chop the crystallised pineapple).
Soften the ice creams by placing
them in the refrigerator. Spoon the
vanilla ice cream into the pan and
smooth it down. Add the chopped
chocolate to the chocolate ice
cream, and ¾ of the chopped
pineapple. Spoon this mixture on
top of the vanilla ice cream. Chop
the nougat into small pieces and
sprinkle it on top of the chocolate
ice cream. Cover the chocolate ice

cream with the remaining 4 wafer
biscuits. Freeze for 3-4 hours, until
firm. Spoon or decorate the
whipped cream over the unmolded
ice cream cake. Decorate with the
reserved pineapple. Serve cut into
slices.

Chocolate Ice Box Cake

PREPARATION TIME: 1 hour,
plus freezing

COOKING TIME: 25-30 minutes

OVEN TEMPERATURE: 375°F

SERVES: 8 people

Melted butter for greasing
7 eggs, separated
6 tblsp vanilla sugar
6 tblsp regular flour
Pinch of salt
Superfine sugar

Filling
12oz semi-sweet chocolate, chopped
   or grated
2½ tblsp strong black coffee
¼ cup brandy
2 egg yolks
5 egg whites, stiffly beaten
½ cup heavy cream, lightly whipped

Frosting
⅔ cup heavy cream
5oz semi-sweet chocolate, chopped or
   grated

Grease and line two 9x12 inch jelly
roll pans with wax paper. Brush the
paper with melted butter and dust
with flour. Beat the egg yolks and
vanilla sugar together until thick
and light; fold in the flour and salt.
Beat the egg whites until stiff but
not dry. Gently fold the beaten egg
whites into the mixture. Divide the
mixture between the two pans.
Bake in a pre-heated oven for 15-20
minutes, or until golden. When the
sponges are baked, spread two tea
towels on a work surface and cover
each one with a sheet of wax paper.
Sprinkle with superfine sugar and
turn the sponges out onto the
sugared paper. Peel off the lining
paper and leave the sponges to
cool. Line the bottom of an 8 inch
spring form cake pan with greased
wax paper. Cut a circle of sponge
from each rectangular sponge to fit
the pan. Put one on top of the
paper lining. Reserve the other.
Cut three strips of sponge, 2 inches
wide, to line the sides of the pan.
Place in position. To make the
filling: put the chocolate, coffee
and brandy into a saucepan and
stir over a low heat until the
chocolate has melted. Leave to
cool. Beat in the egg yolks, and

then gently fold in the beaten egg
whites, taking care not to over-mix.
Finally, fold in the whipped heavy
cream. Pour the mixture into the
sponge-lined cake pan and put the
remaining sponge circle on top as a
lid. Cover the top of the pan with a
plate 8 inches in diameter,
weighted down lightly. Put the cake
pan into the freezer for 2-3 hours,
or chill in the refrigerator for at
least 5 hours. To make the frosting:
pour the cream into a pan and bring
to the boil. Stir in the chocolate
until it melts, and the mixture
thickens. Carefully take the set
cake out of its pan and pour frosting
over it. Open freeze, or refrigerate,
until the frosting has set.

Chocolate Chip Ice Cream

PREPARATION TIME: 30 minutes,
plus freezing time

COOKING TIME: 6-8 minutes

SERVES: 8 people

3½oz semi-sweet chocolate, chopped
   or grated

1¼ cups milk
3 egg yolks
3oz sugar
1¼ cups heavy cream, lightly
   whipped
2½oz finely chopped chocolate

Stir the chopped or grated
chocolate into the milk in a small,
heavy-based saucepan; stir over a
gentle heat until the chocolate
melts. Put the egg yolks into a bowl
with the sugar and beat until thick
and creamy. Add the chocolate
milk and beat. Return the
chocolate mixture to the saucepan
and stir continuously over a
moderate heat until the mixture is
thick and will coat the back of a
spoon. Strain the chocolate custard
into a bowl and cool in the
refrigerator. When quite cold, fold
in the whipped cream. (If you are
using a churn, pour in the mixture
and follow the manufacturer's
instructions, adding the chopped
chocolate at the appropriate stage.)
Pour into ice trays and freeze until
the mixture begins to set around
the edges. Pour into a bowl and
beat. Stir in the chopped
chocolate. Return the ice cream to
the ice trays and freeze for 30
minutes. Repeat the beating and

**Chocolate Ice Cream (above
right) and Nougat Ice Cream
Cake (right).**

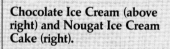

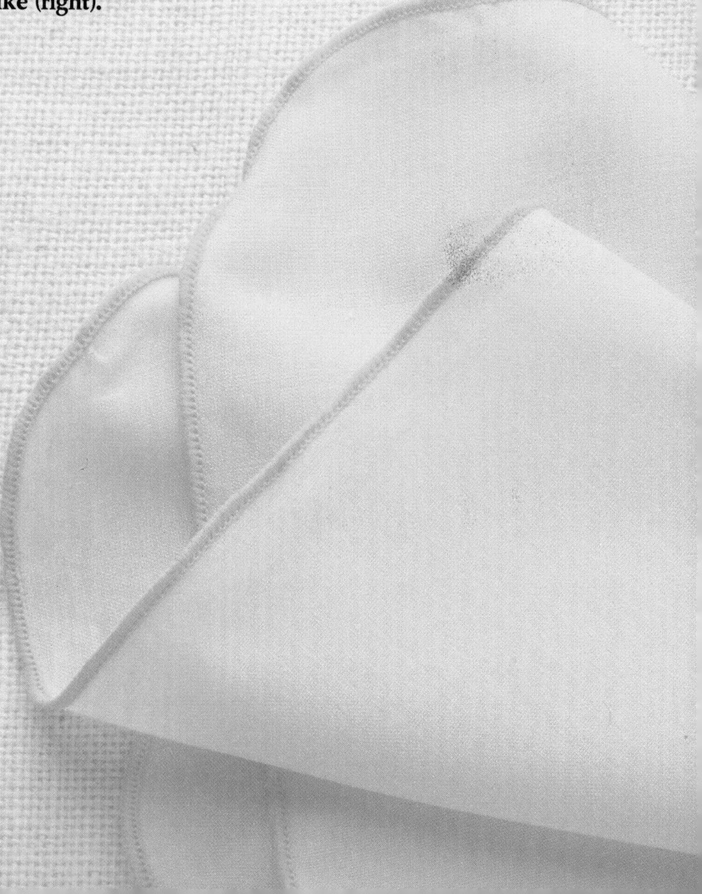

freezing method every 30 minutes, until the ice cream is really thick. Freeze until firm.

Luxury Lace Ice Cream

PREPARATION TIME: 50 minutes, plus freezing

COOKING TIME: 6-8 minutes

SERVES: 6-8 people

1¼ cups light cream
5oz semi-sweet chocolate, chopped or grated
1¼ tsp instant coffee powder
4 egg yolks
½ cup sugar
1¼ cups heavy cream

To Decorate
4oz semi-sweet chocolate, chopped or grated

Put the light cream into a saucepan and heat gently. Add the chocolate and coffee powder and stir until the mixture is smooth, and the chocolate has melted. Beat the egg yolks and sugar until thick, pale and creamy. Continue beating, and slowly pour in the chocolate cream mixture. Return the mixture to the saucepan and stir it over a gentle heat until it reaches coating consistency. Remove from the heat and cool. Whip the cream lightly and fold it into the chocolate mixture. Pour the mixture into a shallow container and freeze it until firm. To make the chocolate lace decoration: put a large cake pan upside down. Smooth a piece of plastic wrap over alternate domed shapes. Melt the plain chocolate and use it to fill a wax pastry bag fitted with a writing tip. Decorate around the edge of each dome and then decorate parallel lines in every direction over the dome, joining up all the lines with circles. Repeat the pattern so that it is "double" in thickness. Chill the chocolate domes until set. Carefully lift them off the cake pan. Keep them chilled until you are ready to serve the ice cream. To serve: put a generous scoop of ice cream into each chocolate lace cup and top it with another cup.

Frozen Chocolate Souffle

PREPARATION TIME: 30 minutes, plus freezing time

COOKING TIME: 15 minutes

SERVES: 6-8 people

This delicate and light chocolate dessert makes an unusual end to a meal.

¼ cup sugar
3 eggs, separated
3½ oz semi-sweet chocolate, melted and cooled
1½ cups heavy cream, lightly whipped

To Decorate
Chocolate scrolls
Confectioner's sugar

Tie a collar of greased wax paper around a 1¼ pint souffle dish,

making sure that it extends at least 2 inches above the rim of the dish. Beat the sugar and egg yolks in a bowl over a pan of simmering water, until thick and light. The mixture should fall off the whisk in ribbons). Remove from the heat and beat in the melted chocolate. Beat until the mixture has cooled. Fold the lightly whipped cream into the chocolate mixture. Beat the egg whites until stiff but not dry; fold lightly into the mixture. Pour the mixture into the prepared souffle dish. Freeze for at least 4 hours. Just before serving, remove the paper collar by gently easing it off. Decorate the top with chocolate scrolls and dust lightly with confectioner's sugar.

Minted Chocolate Chip Gateau

PREPARATION TIME: 25 minutes, plus freezing

COOKING TIME: 20 minutes

OVEN TEMPERATURE: 400°F

SERVES: 6 people

3 large eggs
⅓ cup sugar
¾ cup regular flour, sieved
1 tsp baking powder
Filling
6 scoops chocolate chip ice cream
To decorate
1 box chocolate mint sticks

To make the sponge: beat the eggs and sugar together until they are thick and light in color. Fold the sieved flour lightly but thoroughly into the mixture. Put into a greased and lined shallow loaf pan. Bake in the oven for 20 minutes. Turn out and cool. Slice the cake through into layers; sandwich together with 4 scoops of the ice cream. Spread the remaining ice cream over the sides of the cake, omitting the top; stick on the chocolate mint sticks (you may have to use a piece of string or ribbon to hold them in position). Freeze the cake until firm. Cut the cake into slices to serve.

Iced Lake

PREPARATION TIME: 35 minute, plus freezin

COOKING TIME: 10-15 minutes

OVEN TEMPERATURE: 350°F

SERVES: 6 people

Lemon Ice Cream
Grated rind of 2 lemons
Juice of 3 lemons
¾ cup sugar
1¼ cups heavy cream
1¼ cups milk

Chocolate Cookies
¼ cup butter
¼ cup sugar
1 egg yolk
½ cup regular flour
¼ cup rice flour
1¼ tsp cocoa powder

To Serve
Nouvelle Chocolate Sauce (see recipe)

To make the ice cream: put the lemon rind, juice and sugar into a bowl and stir well. Add the cream and beat until thick. Beat in the milk slowly. Pour the mixture into large freezer container and freeze until slushy. Tip the ice cream into a bowl and beat it until smooth. Re-freeze in its container until firm. To make the cookies: lightly grease a cooky sheet. Cream the butter and sugar together. Add the egg yolk, beat the mixture well. Add the regular flour, rice flour and cocoa and work them well into the mixture. Lightly flour the work surface and roll out the dough. Cut out shapes with animal cutters. Place on a cooky sheet. Bake for 10 15 minutes. Cool on a wire rack. T serve: place scoops of ice cream onto small serving plates and top each one with an animal biscuit. Spoon Nouvelle Chocolate Sauce around each portion.

This page: Iced Lake (top) and **Minted Chocolate Chip Gatea** (bottom).

Facing page: Frozen Chocolate **Souffle** (top) and **Luxury Lace Ice Cream** (bottom).

Cookies and Confections

Chocolate Ravioli

PREPARATION TIME: 30 minutes, plus chilling

MAKES: 25 pieces

1 cup roasted hazelnuts
1¼ tblsp granulated sugar
2½ tblsp melted butter
2oz semi-sweet chocolate melted
1¼ tblsp brandy
9oz white chocolate, melted

Line a square cooky sheet with a rim of tinfoil, making sure that it is smooth and even, with neat corners. Crush the hazelnuts and mix them with the sugar and butter. Stir in the melted dark chocolate and brandy to form a paste. Form into 25 small balls and arrange them in rows over the bottom of the cooky sheet, pressing the balls flat. Pour the melted white chocolate evenly over the small balls so as to cover them completely. Place the tray in the refrigerator until firm. Cut the ravioli into rows with a knife or ravioli cutter and then separate each one.

Chocolate Meringues

PREPARATION TIME: 35 minutes
COOKING TIME: 15-20 minutes
OVEN TEMPERATURE: 350°F
MAKES: about 8

2 egg whites
¾ cup confectioner's sugar, sieved
½ cup nuts

Filling
4oz semi-sweet chocolate, chopped or grated
5 tblsp water
1¼ tblsp strong black coffee
¼ cup butter
2 egg yolks
1¼ tblsp dark rum

Beat the egg whites until stiff and dry. Add the confectioner's sugar a spoonful at a time and continue to beat until very thick. Carefully fold in the chopped nuts; spoon or shape small mounds onto a cooky sheet lined with silicone paper.

Bake for 15-20 minutes. Leave to cool slightly and then transfer onto a wire rack. Gently spoon out a little meringue from the underside of each of the meringues. For the filling: melt the chocolate and stir in the coffee and water; boil the mixture, stirring continuously for 2 minutes. Remove the pan from the heat and allow the mixture to cool; beat the butter into the cooled mixture and blend in the egg yolks and the rum. Refrigerate until the mixture thickens. When cool, spoon it into a pastry bag fitted with a plain tip, and push the filling into the meringues. Sandwich them together in pairs.

This page: Toffee Bars (top left), Chocolate Fudge (top right) and Chocolate Ravioli (bottom).

Facing page: Florentines (top) and Chocolate Meringue Biscuits (bottom).

Chocolate Eggs

PREPARATION TIME: 50 minutes

COOKING TIME: 12-15 minutes

MAKES: 6

6 small eggs
Food coloring
¾ cup heavy cream
10 oz semi-sweet or sweet chocolate, melted
5 tblsp white rum
Sticking plaster or tape

Using a needle, make a small hole in one end of each egg; carefully make a larger hole in the other end. Blow the egg contents out into a bowl. Pour running water into the egg shells and shake them well until clean. Put a little food coloring of your choice into a saucepan of water and boil the egg shells until they take on the color. Dry the shells in a low oven for 5 minutes. Boil the cream and stir it into the melted chocolate. Stir in the rum. Put a small piece of plaster over the smallest hole in each egg shell; fill a pastry bag fitted with a plain tip with the chocolate cream. Fit the tip gently into the egg shell and push in the chocolate cream until full. Clean off any chocolate on the shell and chill. Remove the plasters. These eggs are fun to give as gifts, or use uncolored, as a joke for a chocolate breakfast. Note: stand the eggs in their box to make filling and chilling easier.

Artichoke

PREPARATION TIME: 1 hour 30 minutes, plus setting overnight

MAKES: 1 artichoke, serving 8-10 people

After dinner mints with a difference.

1lb semi-sweet chocolate, chopped or grated
2½ tblsp oil
Few drops of peppermint oil
1 globe artichoke

To Make the Artichoke
2 tblsp sugar
2 tblsp butter
2½ tblsp water
⅓ cup confectioner's sugar, sieved
3 tblsp cocoa powder
A piece of cake the size of the artichoke

Artichoke (above), Chocolate Eggs (right) and Truffles (far right).

Melt the semi-sweet chocolate with the oil and stir occasionally until melted. Cool this mixture slightly and stir in the peppermint oil. Take the leaves off the artichoke; dip the front of each leaf into the melted chocolate and lay them on silicone paper. Leave overnight to set before peeling off the artichoke leaves. To make the frosting: dissolve the sugar in the butter and water over a low heat; remove from the heat and stir in the frosting sugar and the cocoa powder. Cut the cake into a pyramid shape and cover it with some of the cooled frosting. Stick the chocolate artichoke leaves around the cake, in the same order as the real artichoke was assembled. You will need to use some of the frosting to help them to stick. Serve with the peppermint creams at the end of the meal.

Chocolate Fudge

PREPARATION TIME: 35 minutes
COOKING TIME: 10-15 minutes
MAKES: about 1½lbs

This fudge is much easier to make if you have a sugar thermometer, but do not worry if one is not available; the temperature of the fudge can be tested without one.

2 tblsp butter
8oz semi-sweet chocolate, melted
1 cup granulated sugar
1¾ cups canned evaporated milk

To Decorate
3 tblsp cocoa powder or drinking chocolate

If you have a sugar thermometer put it in your saucepan before you start the fudge. Heat the butter, sugar and evaporated milk in the saucepan, stirring continuously, until the sugar has dissolved. Boil the mixture until the thermometer reads 240°F (if you do not have a thermometer, take out a little of the fudge with a small spoon and drop it into a jug of cold water; if it stays in a ball it is ready). Remove the saucepan from the heat and plunge the bottom of the pan into cold water to stop mixture from cooking. After a few minutes beat the fudge until it is thick and grainy. Beat in the melted chocolate. Butter a shallow 12x7 inch cake pan and pour in the fudge. Cool until set. Cut the fudge into squares. Dust the fudge in either cocoa powder or drinking chocolate.

Truffles

PREPARATION TIME: 15 minutes
MAKES: about 10

4oz semi-sweet chocolate, chopped or grated
1¼ tblsp dark rum
2 tblsp unsalted butter
1 egg yolk
½ cup ground almonds
½ cup cake crumbs
2oz chocolate vermicelli

Melt the chocolate with the rum in a small bowl over a saucepan of hot water. Beat in the butter and egg yolk and remove the mixture from

the heat. Stir in the ground almonds and cake crumbs to make a smooth paste. Divide into balls and roll them in the vermicelli until evenly coated.

Dipped Fruit

PREPARATION TIME: 10 minutes, plus drying

MAKES: 1½lb dipped fruit

1½lb prepared fruit (grapes, strawberries, etc.)
Melted plain chocolate

Wash the fruits, but leave the stems on them if possible. Holding each piece of fruit by the stem, dip into the melted chocolate, leaving the top section uncovered. Allow any excess to run off and leave to set on a tray lined with silicone paper.

Chocolate Meringue Cookies

PREPARATION TIME: 20 minutes

COOKING TIME: 15-20 minutes

OVEN TEMPERATURE: 350°F

MAKES: about 10

½ cup butter or margarine
¼ cup sugar
1 egg yolk
¼ cup ground almonds
1½ cups regular flour

Filling
4oz semi-sweet chocolate
1 tblsp butter

Meringue Topping
For meringue ingredients see
Chocolate Meringues recipe

Grease a cooky sheet and line with silicone paper. Cream the butter or margarine and sugar together; add the egg yolk and beat well. Add the ground almonds and flour and mix well. Knead the mixture and roll it out thinly. Cut into rounds using a 2½ inch cutter. Place the rounds on the prepared cooky sheet and bake for 15-20 minutes. Make up the meringue mixture. Shape into 1 inch swirls on a cooky sheet lined with silicone paper. Follow the baking instructions for chocolate meringues. When cool, gently ease them off the cooky sheet. To make up the filling: melt the chocolate with the butter over a gentle heat.

Mix well and spread over the top of each of the almond cookies. Top each one with a meringue and leave until set.

Florentines

PREPARATION TIME: 15 minutes

COOKING TIME: 8-10 minutes

OVEN TEMPERATURE: 350°F

MAKES: 12

⅓ cup butter
⅓ cup corn syrup
⅔ cup flaked almonds, chopped
¼ cup regular flour
2 tblsp chopped mixed peel
4 tblsp candied cherries, chopped
1¼ tsp lemon juice
4oz semi-sweet chocolate, chopped or grated

Line a cooky sheet with silicone paper. Melt the butter and syrup together in a small saucepan. Stir in the almonds, flour, mixed peel, cherries and lemon juice. Put small spoonfuls of the mixture onto the prepared cooky sheet. Keep them well apart and flatten with a fork. Bake in a pre-heated oven for 8-10 minutes. Remove the Florentines carefully to a wire rack to cool. Melt the chocolate in a bowl over a pan of hot water. Spread over the

flat side of each Florentine. Place the cookies chocolate sides uppermost, and mark the liquid chocolate with wavy lines, using a fork. Leave until set.

Toffee Bars

PREPARATION TIME: 40 minutes

COOKING TIME: 25-30 minutes

OVEN TEMPERATURE: 350°F

MAKES: 15 bars

Cooky Base
½ cup butter
¼ cup sugar
1½ cups regular flour, sieved

Toffee Caramel
½ cup butter or margarine
¼ cup sugar
2½ tblsp golden syrup
⅔ cup condensed milk

Chocolate Topping
4oz semi-sweet chocolate
1 tblsp butter

For the cooky base: cream the butter and sugar together until light and fluffy. Add the flour and knead until smooth. Press the dough into a greased, 8 inch square shallow cake pan, and prick with a fork. Bake in a pre-heated oven for

25-30 minutes. Cool. Put the ingredients for the toffee caramel into a small saucepan and stir until dissolved; bring slowly to the boil, and cook stirring for 5-7 minutes. Cool slightly and then spread over the cooky base. Leave to set. For the topping: melt the chocolate with the butter over a low heat; spread it carefully over the toffee. Leave it to set and cut into fingers.

Chocolate Muesli

PREPARATION TIME: 25 minutes

COOKING TIME: 10-12 minutes

OVEN TEMPERATURE: 375°F

MAKES: about 12

½ cup margarine or butter
½ cup sugar
1 egg, beaten
Few drops vanilla essence
1 cup regular flour, sieved
½ tsp bicarbonate of soda
¼ cup rolled oats
⅓ cup cocoa powder

Chocolate Coating
4oz semi-sweet chocolate, chopped or grated
1 tblsp butter

Beat the margarine or butter with the sugar until light and fluffy. Beat in the egg, adding the essence, flour and bicarbonate of soda. Stir in the oats and the cocoa powder. Spread the mixture onto a lightly greased cooky sheet, and mark out into bars with a knife. Bake for 10-12 minutes until lightly browned. Re-mark with a sharp knife and cool on a wire rack. To make the chocolate coating: melt the chocolate and butter together and pour evenly over the bars. Separate the bars when set.

This page: Chocolate Meringues (top) and Dipped Fruit (bottom).

Facing page: Praline Orange Log (top), Chocolate Muesli (center right) and Mint Cream (bottom left).

Chocolate Chip Cookies

PREPARATION TIME:	15 minutes, plus chilling
COOKING TIME:	10-12 minutes
OVEN TEMPERATURE:	350°F
MAKES:	about 30

2 cups regular flour
Pinch of salt
10 tblsp butter
½ cup sugar
1 egg, lightly beaten
2oz semi-sweet chocolate, grated

Sieve the flour and salt into a mixing bowl. Cut the butter into the flour and cut in until the mixture looks like breadcrumbs. Stir the sugar into the mixture. Add the egg and mix to a stiff dough. Knead the grated chocolate into the dough. Chill the dough for 30 minutes. Roll out the dough and cut into 2 inch rounds with a plain cutter. Grease a cooky sheet and put the rounds on it, placing them well apart. Prick the rounds with a fork. Bake in a pre-heated oven for 10-12 minutes until golden. Cool on a wire rack.

Chocolate Crunch

PREPARATION TIME:	20 minutes, plus chilling
MAKES:	1 1lb loaf

4oz chocolate shortbread finger cookies
¼ cup whole hazelnuts
½ cup firm margarine
⅓ cup sugar
2½ tblsp cocoa powder
1 egg, beaten
7 tblsp white raisins

To Decorate
Confectioner's sugar

Line a 1lb loaf pan with plastic wrap. Chop up the shortbread fingers. Brown the hazelnuts and rub off the skins. Put the margarine and sugar into a small saucepan and stir over a low heat until the sugar dissolves. Stir the cocoa into the mixture, and remove from the heat. Stir in the egg, hazelnuts, white raisins and chopped cookies. Pour the mixture into the lined pan and smooth it level. Chill until set. Dust with confectioner's sugar and serve cut in slices.

Chocolate Palmiers

PREPARATION TIME:	30 minutes
COOKING TIME:	12-15 minutes
OVEN TEMPERATURE:	425°F
MAKES:	6

8oz puff pastry
Superfine sugar
3oz semi-sweet chocolate, coarsely grated

To decorate
¾ cup heavy cream, whipped
2oz strawberries, halved
Confectioners sugar for dusting

Roll out the pastry on a well-sugared surface to a rectangle measuring approximately 12x10 inches. Sprinkle with the chocolate and press down with a rolling pin. Take the shorter edge of the pastry and roll it up to the center. Roll the opposite side to meet it at the center. Moisten with water and press together the adjoining rolls. Cut into ½ inch slices and place them cut side down on a dampened cooky sheet. Keep them well apart and flatten them a little. Bake in a pre-heated oven for 12-15 minutes, until puffed and golden. (Turn the palmiers over once they begin to brown.) Cool them on a wire rack. Whip the cream and use it to fill a pastry bag fitted with a ½ inch fluted tip. Shape swirls of cream on half of the palmiers and arrange the fruit on top of the cream. Use the other palmiers to sandwich the fruit. Sprinkle with confectioner's sugar.

Praline Orange Log

PREPARATION TIME:	20-25 minutes, plus chilling
COOKING TIME:	30-35 minutes
OVEN TEMPERATURE:	350°F
MAKES:	30 slices

6oz semi-sweet chocolate, chopped or grated
1¼ tblsp strong black coffee
2 tblsp sugar
1¼ tblsp orange liqueur
⅓ cup butter
2 egg yolks

Praline
1½ cups shelled nuts (see below)
1 cup granulated sugar
⅓ cup water
1 egg white, beaten

Use either almonds, hazelnuts, walnuts or pistachio nuts. Use the nuts chopped or whole, with or without the skins, toasted or plain. For praline powder, the nuts must be peeled.

Melt the chocolate in a bowl with the coffee, sugar, orange liqueur and butter, over a low heat. Remove from the heat and allow to cool thoroughly. Stir in the egg yolks. Chill for 3½-4 hours. To make the praline: put the nuts on a cooky sheet and warm them in the oven for 10 minutes. Butter a marble slab or large cooky sheet. Put the sugar and water into a small, heavy saucepan, stirring until the sugar has dissolved. Bring to the boil and boil until the sugar caramelizes; remove from the heat and plunge the base of the pan into cold water to halt the cooking process. Stir in the nuts. Pour onto the marble or onto a cooky sheet. Spread out and leave until set and hard. Put the praline into a strong plastic bag and crush with a rolling pin. To make praline powder, grind it in a coffee grinder. Shape the chilled chocolate mixture into a log, 2 inches in diameter. Brush the log with the beaten egg white and roll gently in the crushed praline, pressing firmly with the hands to help the praline stick. Chill the log until very firm. Cut into slices about ¼ inch thick.

Chocolate Crunch (top right), Chocolate Palmiers (center left) and Chocolate Chip Cookies (bottom).

Mint Creams

PREPARATION TIME: 20 minutes, plus setting overnight

MAKES: about 16

The white of 1 egg
¼ tsp peppermint essence
2¼ cups confectioner's sugar
4oz semi-sweet chocolate, chopped or grated

Beat the egg white and essence together in a bowl and gradually add the confectioner's sugar. Lightly dust the work surface with extra confectioner's sugar and knead the peppermint frosting until smooth. Using plenty of extra icing sugar, roll out the frosting to a thickness of about ¼ inch and cut out shapes with a 1½ inch cutter, either fluted or plain. Place the shaped mints on a cooky sheet lined with wax paper, and leave them in a warm place to dry out, preferably overnight. Melt the chocolate; dip the mints in so that half is coated in chocolate. Shake off any excess chocolate and place the mints on a sheet of buttered wax paper or foil until set.

Dominoes

PREPARATION TIME: 25 minutes

COOKING TIME: 10-15 minutes

OVEN TEMPERATURE: 350°F

MAKES: about 14

½ cup butter or margarine
½ cup sugar
1 egg, beaten
2¼ cups regular flour
3 tblsp cocoa powder
Salt

Butter Frosting
⅓ cup butter
1 cup + 2 tblsp confectioner's sugar, sieved
Few drops of vanilla essence

Cream the butter and sugar together and add the egg. Sieve the flour, cocoa powder and salt together and work into the butter mixture. Knead the dough and roll it out between two sheets of wax paper. Cut out rectangles, about 1¼x2¾ inches. Mark a line across the center of the biscuits using a skewer. Bake the cookies on a

greased cooky sheet for 10-15 minutes. Cool them on a wire rack. To make the frosting: soften the butter and beat in the frosting sugar. You may need to add a few drops of hot water if the frosting is too firm. Add vanilla essence to taste. If you want to sandwich the cookies together, do so with a little of the butter frosting. Decorate the top of the dominoes with dots, using a pastry bag fitted with a plain tip and filled with the remaining butter frosting.

Zigzag Shortbread

PREPARATION TIME: 20 minutes

COOKING TIME: 30-35 minutes

OVEN TEMPERATURE: 325°F

MAKES: about 14 fingers

1¼ cups regular flour
¼ cup sugar
½ cup butter
1¼ tblsp cocoa powder
1¼ tblsp drinking chocolate

Grease a 7 inch square cake pan. Sieve the flour into a bowl, reserving ½oz. Add the sugar. Cut in the butter until it forms a crumble texture. Divide the

mixture in half; add the cocoa and the drinking chocolate to one half. Add the remaining flour to the other half. Knead both mixtures to doughs. Turn the chocolate dough onto a lightly floured surface. Roll out and cut into strips 1½ inches wide. Do the same with the plain dough. Lay the strips alternately in the pan, in a diagonal pattern, easing them in so that they fit. Bake until lightly crisp but not brown, for 30-35 minutes. Mark out into fingers and leave to cool in the pan. Note: the shortbread trimmings can be cut into small shapes and baked separately for 5 minutes.

Chocolate Whirls

PREPARATION TIME: 10 minutes

COOKING TIME: 15 minutes

OVEN TEMPERATURE: 350°F

MAKES: 10

¼ cup butter or margarine
2 tblsp brown sugar
1¼ tblsp molasses
1 tsp cocoa powder
Pinch of salt
1 cup regular flour

1¼ tsp baking powder
10 hazelnuts

Grease a cooky sheet. Put the butter and sugar into a mixing bowl and beat until soft and creamy. Add the molasses and stir well. Sieve the cocoa powder, flour and salt together and knead into the molasses mixture. Spoon the mixture into small balls on a floured work surface. Roll the balls into long sausage shapes; curve round one end and continue winding the rest of the sausage round so you have a Catherine wheel shape. Place the "wheels" on the cooky sheet; push a hazelnut into the center of each one. Bake for 15 minutes. Cool on a wire rack

This page: Chocolate Whirls (left), Zigzag Shortbread (center) and Dominoes (right).

Facing page: Iced Chocolate (left) and Chocolate Egg Cream Soda (right).

Drinks and Sauces

₋ed Chocolate

PREPARATION TIME: 5 minutes,
plus chilling

COOKING TIME: 15 minutes

MAKES: 8-10 drinks

₋ cup granulated sugar
₋cup water
₋½ tblsp cocoa powder
₋chilled milk

₋ut the sugar and water into a
₋eavy-based saucepan and stir over
₋ moderate heat until the sugar
₋issolves. Brush off any sugar
₋rystals that may form on the
₋side of the pan with a pastry
₋rush dipped in cold water. Raise
₋he heat and boil the syrup until it
₋pins fine threads from a spoon or
₋ork. Remove from the heat. Add
₋he cocoa powder and stir until
₋ell mixed over a low heat. Cool
₋he chocolate syrup and chill in the
₋efrigerator until required. To make
₋he drink: put 1 tblsp chilled syrup
₋to a jug or blender with 1¼ cups
₋hilled milk and stir or blend until
₋lended. Pour the chocolate drink
₋ver ice cubes in chilled glasses.

₋ittersweet Butter ₋ream

PREPARATION TIME: 15 minutes

MAKES: 1¾ cups

₋oz unsweetened chocolate
₋½ cups butter softened
₋½ cups sugar
₋ tsp vanilla essence
₋ eggs
₋ tblsp cocoa powder
₋ tsp instant coffee powder
₋ tsp dark rum
₋inch of salt

₋Melt the chocolate. Beat the butter
₋ntil creamy and add the sugar and
₋anilla. Add the eggs, one at a time,
₋eating well after each addition.
₋tir cocoa and coffee powder into
₋he melted chocolate and add it to
₋he buttercream. Stir in the rum
₋nd salt, making sure that all the
₋ngredients are well incorporated.
₋Jse to fill Chocolate Raspberry
₋orte, or other chocolate recipe.

Banana Shake

PREPARATION TIME: 10 minutes

MAKES: 1 drink

3 tblsp chocolate ice cream
2 tblsp drinking chocolate powder
⅔ cup milk
1 banana
Ice cubes

Blend together all the ingredients in a blender or food processor, or beat with a hand whisk (if using a hand whisk, mash the banana first). Serve in a tall glass with ice cubes.

Chocolate Butter Sauce

PREPARATION TIME: 5 minutes

COOKING TIME: 10 minutes

MAKES: 1¾ cups

1 cup water
8oz semi-sweet chocolate, chopped or grated
1 tblsp brandy
7 tblsp butter, cut into small pieces

Put the water, chocolate and brandy into a saucepan. Stir over a low heat until the chocolate has melted. The mixture should be smooth. Remove from the heat and slowly stir in the butter until it melts. The sauce should then become thick and glossy. This sauce can be served hot or cold.

Praline Sauce

PREPARATION TIME: 40 minutes, including making of praline

MAKES: about 1¼ cups

1 tblsp cocoa powder
6oz canned evaporated milk
3oz semi-sweet chocolate, chopped or grated
5 tblsp crushed praline (see recipe)

Beat together the cocoa and evaporated milk in a small saucepan. Heat the mixture and bring it to the boil. Remove the pan from the heat and stir in the chocolate. Return to the heat and continue stirring over a gentle heat until the chocolate has melted. Add the praline.

Chocolate Toffee Sauce

PREPARATION TIME: 10 minutes

COOKING TIME: 15 minutes

MAKES: about 1¼ cups

4oz semi-sweet chocolate, chopped or grated
⅓ cup water
¼ cup granulated sugar
4 tblsp chilled unsalted butter
1 tsp vanilla essence
8oz nut brittle, broken into small chunks

Using a small, heavy-based saucepan, gently heat the chocolate and water until the chocolate has melted. Stir continuously. Stir in the sugar and continue to heat gently for 2 minutes, until the sugar has dissolved and the mixture has thickened. Remove the sauce from the heat and beat in the butter. Stir in the vanilla and the broken nut brittle. Serve hot. This sauce can be kept in the refrigerator for a few days. To serve warm, heat it gently to a pouring consistency.

Peppermint Sauce

PREPARATION TIME: 15 minutes

MAKES: about 1 cup

3oz chocolate covered peppermint creams
⅔ cup light cream

Break up the peppermint creams and melt over a pan of hot water. Remove from the heat and slowly stir in the cream. Serve the sauce hot or cold with ice cream.

This page: Praline Sauce – shown with Nougat Slice – (top), Bitter Chocolate Sauce – shown with Cherries – (center right) and Chocolate Butter Sauce (bottom left).

Facing page: Hot Fudge Sauce (left) and Chocolate Toffee Sauce (right).

Chocolate Custard

PREPARATION TIME: 10 minutes

COOKING TIME: 3 minutes

MAKES: about 2½ cups

4 egg yolks
¼ cup sugar
2 cups milk
4oz semi-sweet chocolate, chopped or
    grated

Heat the milk until very hot. Add the chocolate and stir until melted. Beat the egg yolks and sugar together until pale and creamy. Slowly pour the milk onto the egg mixture and blend. Return mixture to pan and heat over medium heat, stirring constantly, until sauce thickens. Serve hot.

Bitter Chocolate Sauce

PREPARATION TIME: 5 minutes

COOKING TIME: 15 minutes

MAKES: 1 cup

4 tblsp strong black coffee
4oz semi-sweet chocolate, chopped or
    grated
½ cup heavy cream
⅓ cup apricot jam

Put all the ingredients into a small, heavy-based pan. Stir continuously over a low heat until smooth.

Honey Nut Spread (above), Chocolate Custard – shown with Steamed Pudding – (center right) and Bittersweet Butter Cream (far right).

Nouvelle Sauce

PREPARATION TIME: 10 minutes

COOKING TIME: 5 minutes

MAKES: 1¾ cups

This is a thin chocolate sauce which is served slightly cooled.

8oz semi-sweet chocolate, chopped or grated
½ cup granulated sugar
2 cups water
2½ tsp brandy

Melt the chocolate with the sugar and water; simmer for 4-5 minutes, stirring continuously. Remove the pan from the heat and let the chocolate mixture cool. Stir in the brandy. Strain the sauce and serve.

Honey Nut Spread

PREPARATION TIME: 10 minutes

MAKES: about 6oz

¼ cup butter, softened
1¼ tblsp cocoa powder
2 tsp orange liqueur
2½ tblsp honey
3 tblsp confectioner's sugar
½ cup nuts, chopped

Cream the butter with the cocoa powder and the orange liqueur; beat in the honey and the confectioner's sugar, and then fold in the nuts. This spread is now ready to serve on hot toasted crumpets, or muffins, and is delicious with pancakes.

Chocolate Cream Sauce

PREPARATION TIME: 5 minutes

COOKING TIME: 10-15 minutes

MAKES: 1¾ cups

1¼ cups heavy cream
1 tblsp brandy
1 tblsp strong black coffee
8oz semi-sweet chocolate, chopped or grated

Pour the cream, brandy and coffee into a small, heavy-based saucepan and bring to the boil. Remove from the heat and add the chopped chocolate. Stir the chocolate until it melts and the sauce is smooth. Serve this sauce hot or cold.

Cocoa Rum

PREPARATION TIME: 5 minutes

MAKES: 1 drink

½oz semi-sweet chocolate, chopped or grated
⅔ cup milk
1 tblsp rum
1 tblsp whipped cream
Grated nutmeg

Put the chocolate and milk into a saucepan and bring it to the boil. Stir the chocolate milk a few times, and then remove it from the heat. Beat in the rum and pour into a heatproof glass. Put a spoonful of cream on the top and sprinkle with grated nutmeg.

Malted Chocolate Shake

PREPARATION TIME: 10 minutes, plus chilling

COOKING TIME: 5 minutes

MAKES: 2 drinks

¼ cup soft brown sugar
4½ tblsp cocoa powder
1¼ cups milk
2 tblsp vanilla ice cream
1 tblsp whiskey

Put all the ingredients except the whiskey and ice cream into a saucepan and mix well. Bring gently to the boil. Cook gently for 5 minutes, stirring frequently. Remove from the heat and leave to cool. Beat in the ice cream. Cover and chill in the refrigerator until required. Pour into two glasses and add the whiskey.

Chocolate Egg Cream Soda

PREPARATION TIME: 8 minutes

MAKES: 2 drinks

2oz semi-sweet chocolate, melted
1 egg
1¼ cups full cream milk
2 scoops chocolate ice cream
Chilled soda water
2 scoops vanilla ice cream

Put two tall glasses in the freezer until they are frosted. Put the melted chocolate, egg, milk and chocolate ice cream into the blender; blend for 1 minute. Divide this mixture between two glasses; add a scoop of vanilla ice cream to each one and top up with chilled soda water. Serve while it is still frothing.

Hot Fudge Sauce

PREPARATION TIME: 10 minutes

COOKING TIME: 10 minutes

MAKES: about 1¾ cups

10 tblsp unsalted butter
6 tblsp cocoa powder
2oz semi-sweet chocolate, chopped or grated
⅓ cup granulated sugar
½ cup evaporated milk
Pinch of salt
A few drops of vanilla essence

Melt the butter in a small, heavy-based saucepan. Remove from heat and add the cocoa powder. Beat until smooth. Stir in the chopped chocolate, sugar and evaporated milk; bring to the boil over a moderate heat, stirring continuously. Remove the sauce from the heat and stir in the salt and vanilla essence. This sauce will keep in the refrigerator for 2-3 days.

Coffolate

PREPARATION TIME: 10 minutes plus chilling time

COOKING TIME: about 15 minutes

MAKES: 4 drinks

1 tblsp cornstarch
1¾ cups boiling coffee
1¾ cups hot milk
2oz semi-sweet chocolate, chopped or grated
½ tsp ground cinnamon
½ cup sugar

To Decorate
Whipped cream

Mix the cornstarch to a paste with a little of the coffee. Place the hot milk in a bowl over a pan of simmering water (or into a double boiler). Mix in the cornstarch paste and stir well. Add the chocolate, cinnamon, sugar and remaining coffee. Simmer the mixture for 15 minutes, beating with a whisk; cool and chill. Serve in tall glasses with the cream to decorate.

This page, top picture: Cocoa Rum (left) and Coffolate (right). Bottom picture: Nouvelle Sauce (top left), Chocolate Cream Sauce (top right) and Peppermint Sauce – shown with Pear Pie – (bottom).

Facing page: Malted Chocolate Shake (left) and Banana Shake (right).

Index